DON'T BLINK

A KATE CARPENTER THRILLER

VANESSA ROBERTSON

WILD JUSTICE PRESS

1

Frost crunched beneath the soles of my leather boots as I walked through the St. Petersburg park. It was quiet, the sun was pale and cold, and watching from behind my sunglasses, I felt a steady hum of adrenaline sharpened by a needle of fear.

A few couples ambled along the paths, snapping photos and pointing at views. I slowed my pace, watching until I was sure they were only interested in each other and oblivious to the less recreational activities going on around them. A man with a camera passed me, his nod almost imperceptible, as was the shadow of the gun beneath his jacket.

Two elderly babushkas in fur coats and hats were taking a constitutional before what I guessed would be a morning of tea and gossip in one of the local cafes. I didn't think they were gangsters in disguise because they had the walk right. No-one ever gets the walk right; shoulders insufficiently rounded by age, their stride a little too fast or too sure. No, I was sure these two were just little old ladies.

Tensing at a sound like a rifle-crack nearby, my left hand tightened on the grip of the Beretta in my pocket. My shooting skills were scant, gained in one session at an American range and limited mostly to instructions on how not to injure myself. Given that, I hoped I'd never need that Beretta.

"It's okay, Kate, only a twig. Keep walking. Just Tommo not looking where he's putting his size elevens." The low voice in my left ear was calm, amused even.

Strolling towards the canal, the laptop bag heavy on my shoulder, I saw a man in a fur hat and overcoat sitting on an iron bench facing the railings. He was watching the ducks as they skidded on the ice.

My quarry.

I took a seat next to him, on his left so I could keep my hand on the gun and he wouldn't see my earpiece. Placing my bag on the ground between us, I pretended to watch the ducks too.

"It's a bitter morning, isn't it?" I spoke lightly, the typical Brit who would prefer to make a banal comment about the weather rather than sit in silence.

"Yes. Unexpectedly so." He had only the barest hint of an accent.

"Such a beautiful view. Like a Monet snow scene."

A drake slipped, tumbling beak over tail, and I smiled, despite the anticipation making my heart race. On the other side of the canal, a tall fair-haired man loitering near a bridge with a camera in his hand glanced in our direction. The casual observer wouldn't have noticed the way his eyes scanned the trees or the outline of the gun under his black jacket. But my companion on the bench noticed. I sensed him turn towards me. He knew who I was now.

"You have it?" A suspicious note in his voice.

"Of course. And do you?" I was still smiling, watching as

the clumsy duck regained his feet and shook his feathers back into place.

"Naturally." The man sounded defensive.

"Super. Then I should get going. It's too cold to sit here any longer." Without letting my polite, business-like expression slip, I got to my feet, picked up the leather briefcase positioned next to my laptop bag, and turned to look at the delivery man for the first time. He was clean-shaven and powerfully built, running a little to seed now as he settled into middle age. But despite his carefully generic appearance, I'd know him again.

Nodding a farewell, I started to walk back across the park. As always, it crossed my mind that today might be the day a bullet would get me from a messenger unaware or uncaring of the bodyguards circling me. But I kept walking.

The man from across the canal, Pete, was on my left now, twenty feet away and drawing closer. The photographer I'd spotted earlier was on my other side, another man ahead, one more behind. All armed and willing to be ruthless if they felt I was at risk.

I left by the wrought-iron gates, my minders in a tight group around me, and paused at the open door of a black Range Rover so that an eager spaniel could sniff the briefcase.

Then I heard the shot.

"Get in!"

Heart pounding, I shook off one of my guards, resisting his attempt to bundle me into the safety of the car. A hand on the gates, I looked back towards the canal. The man I'd been speaking to only two minutes earlier was slumped forward on the bench. As he fell to the ground, I saw a figure in a fur coat bend to retrieve the laptop bag and then walk away. Her shoulders were a little hunched with age, her feet a little cautious on the ice. And there was a gun in her right hand.

"Get in the car or I'll pick you up and put you in." Pete's mouth was close by my ear, one hand tight on my upper arm, weapon drawn, like those of my other minders. To argue with him was futile, so I climbed in, trying to regain my composure. Pete got into the front passenger seat and I saw him exchange a sharp look and a few words of Russian with the driver who just shrugged in response. The other men took their seats in identical vehicles positioned in front and behind. I could sense the driver itching to get moving, engine already running, but he waited for his instructions.

The locks closed with a clunk and, shielded by tinted windows and armour-plating, I took some deep breaths, feeling my heart rate slow again, and willing my hands not to shake. Only then, did I take my gloves and sunglasses off and unsnap the catches of the briefcase on my knee. I took out my tiny halogen torch and drew another deep breath as I bent to examine the contents. I had my suspicions as to who was behind the shooting, but for now, I just needed to inspect the painting and finish my job.

The vibrant colours of the tiny Cézanne canvas glowed. Unmistakably the original artwork and seemingly unharmed by its recent adventures, it sang to me. Bending over, shining my torch to see the thickness and layering of the oil paint's application, I saw the details I'd memorised from a hundred photographs. I examined the pencil marks and gallery labels on the reverse and the narrow edges where the canvas was folded around its wooden battens, only visible now because the frame still hung in the Parisian home from which it had been stolen. The torch's beam showed up each identifying smudge and line.

"Welcome back, gorgeous." I whispered, wishing I could take it home to hang on my wall where I could admire it every day. Holding the Cézanne in my hands, I couldn't help smiling, despite events of the last few minutes. With a twinge of regret, I replaced it in the briefcase and closed the catches.

"All right, Kate?" I felt Pete's hand on my knee. I glanced up at him, an eyebrow raised. With the smallest of smiles, he removed his hand.

"It's fine. Perfect." I turned to the man sitting beside me in the car. "It's the one."

Alex smiled back, less broadly it had to be said. Although my job was over, he still needed to keep the painting safe for a little longer.

He pressed a button on his walkie-talkie and muttered something in Russian, presumably standing down other watchers in the park I'd been unaware of, even though my minders would have spotted them. Watchers whose priorities were the Cézanne and, unfortunately for the man on the bench, the half-million dollars of ransom money I'd handed over in return for this painting that I'd chased all over Europe. Watchers who wanted both painting and cash.

"That's excellent, Miss Carpenter." Alex turned to me. "Thank you for all your efforts. My employer will be delighted to have the artwork back." Alex was a slight man, efficient and polite and no doubt under-appreciated by his employer. The Alexes of the world I moved in always were.

"So he should be, it's beautiful. He's a lucky man." I pulled my gloves on briskly, wanting to be on my way. I was a little taken aback at Alex's callousness as he ignored the fact that there was a corpse a few hundred yards away. "Now, I need to get home. Is the plane ready?"

"It is."

"Good. Then let's go. I'll let your employer have an invoice for my expenses." I looked out of the window at the park gates, trying again to push away the image of the man falling from the bench.

Alex tapped the driver on the shoulder and he pulled out into the traffic, the other cars taking positions behind and ahead of us. As we sped through the city, I glimpsed gilded domes sprinkled with snow and grand palaces, a city and culture I would have liked more time to explore. Opening the case, I gazed again at the Cézanne, soon to return to the privacy of its fortress, albeit a fortress that had been breached once already.

At the terminal building, I said goodbye to Alex and watched as the three black cars swept away with their precious cargo. From the VIP area I could see two planes waiting on the tarmac. One shiny and sleek to take me home to Edinburgh and a larger, rather battered workhorse that would ferry Pete and his team back to the Middle East where they were currently employed to look after the safety of news crews in Syria.

Pete and I had worked together a few times since we met about year and a half ago. We first crossed paths when an insurance underwriter was particularly keen for me to recover a painting from somewhere I didn't feel safe going. He put me in touch with Pete, and he and his team of fellow former Special Forces soldiers came along to keep me and the van Gogh safe. After that, it had been a regular arrangement whenever I felt I needed protection.

After being ushered through the lounge to one of the private meeting rooms to divest ourselves of items that weren't best waved around publicly, I handed my little Beretta to Pete.

"You okay?" He took the gun and made it safe.

"I'm fine. Or I will be. I don't like how that went, though. It was unnecessary and it's not how I work. That poor man. If another of Navarro's paintings goes walkabout he can hire someone else to find it." Shaken, I just wanted to go home, back to somewhere I didn't need minders to protect me. "Had you spotted her?"

"Yes." Pete shrugged. "But I didn't consider her a threat to you. And your safety is my job. I'm not there to worry about anybody else. Smart though; few people would have suspected the old lady."

"I didn't." That made me cross too. I'd been doing this long enough to know not to underestimate anyone.

Taking off my coat, I ripped open the Velcro of my Kevlar vest and took out my earpiece, turning and lifting my dark brown hair so that Pete could remove the wire from my back. His hands were warm, despite the St Petersburg temperatures, but I winced as he ripped the tape from my skin.

"Wimp," he whispered, his breath stirring the fine hairs on the nape of my neck.

"You're such a gentleman. Thanks."

"Anytime. It's good to see you. If only fleetingly." His hands lingered a little as he smoothed down the shoulders of my cashmere jersey.

"It's been a while." I turned to look at him.

"Hasn't it just?" Pete leaned in, his voice low. "I don't have to return with the other guys. I could easily come to Edinburgh. You know, if you haven't any plans for the next couple of days?" He stroked a strand of hair back from my face just as he had so many times before and my pulse quickened despite myself. He smiled as if he could tell.

"You know my answer to that, Pete."

"That's a shame." His hazel eyes remained intent on mine. "But I'm still hopeful you'll come to your senses one day."

"Not going to happen, darling. Thanks for today." I swung my bag onto my shoulder and kissed his cheek, turning to leave and walk away. I was keen to sort out the formalities and be on my way home. As I left the room, I raised a hand in farewell, knowing he was still watching me.

To be honest, it probably would happen, if and when I was single again, and we both knew it. There was a lot of history between Pete and me, all of it happy, and although we moved on for the right reasons, I missed him sometimes. But we parted on good terms and I still trusted him with my life. I wondered how many people could say that about their ex-lovers. For now though, I put temptation aside and reminded myself of all the reasons Pete wasn't hopping on my plane.

2

Try as I might, I couldn't shake visions of the dead man or the babushka with the gun from my mind. I'd got up early that morning to go to St Petersburg, but each time sleep beckoned on the flight home, I woke with a start, heart pounding. Although people had pulled weapons in the past in a fit of bravado, I'd never seen anyone killed or injured before. I was both annoyed and scared that I'd been complacent enough to dismiss the killer as a gossipy old lady. It was all very well for Pete to reassure me that he and his team had spotted her and that she would never have had a chance to get near me, but I shouldn't have underestimated her.

Getting back to my flat, a horizontal slice of a Georgian townhouse in Edinburgh's New Town, was a relief. This was my sanctuary, just as I liked it, from the bookcases covering a whole wall of the drawing room, to the kitchen that had changed little in fifty years and where my china and glasses were neatly lined up on the shelves of the massive dresser. The table, left behind by the previous owners and probably the ones before them, where friends and I put the world to rights over takeaways and plenty of wine, was so big that I guessed it could only be removed by dismantling it.

Also left behind by the flat's previous owners was Arthur the cat. When I first discovered him and the Paddington Bear-style request to look after him, I hadn't minded too much, rather liking the idea of a furry flatmate to come home to.

That was a notion swiftly dispelled by Arthur, who was waiting in the hall that afternoon with his usual air of low-level malevolence. Following him to the kitchen where he looked pointedly at his kibble-filled bowl, I put down the contents of one of the vile-smelling pouches that he considered a more suitable offering and tickled him under the chin. He bit me. It had turned out that I wasn't a cat person after all and he wasn't a cat that was keen on people, but because I was too soft-hearted to take him to the Cat and Dog Home we appeared to be stuck with each other.

It wasn't an evening for culture or deep thought, so after peeling off my thermals and the leftover scraps of tape that had held the wire for my earpiece, I put on leggings and a saggy old cardigan and rootled through the fridge for the makings of dinner. There was some leftover Bolognese that smelt okay and so I made pasta and poured a glass of red wine, taking it through to the sitting room where I lit a fire and shut out the darkness by folding the shutters across the three tall windows.

Half an hour into something sufficiently mindless on TV and halfway down my wine, I felt better. At the very least, I'd stopped thinking about the dead man and wondering whether I could have done anything to prevent his death, maybe even given him some warning. But how could I have known?

My phone rang and there was Kolya, all piercing blue eyes and a smile that could light up a whole theatre.

"Hi." I wasn't in the mood for conversation and even I could hear it in my voice.

"Hello, my darling. How was Paris?"

"Oh, cold and wet. I didn't see much of it between the airport and the gallery." I felt a pang of guilt at lying to him about where I'd been and what I'd been doing, but now was not the time to put him straight. "I'm back home now, curled up with a fire going."

"I wish I was with you."

"You really don't. I'm tired and not great company."

"We'll have another weekend in Paris soon, no?"

"I'd like that. Are you still coming to London next week?"

"Yes, on Tuesday. I have meetings but I'll be free by dinner."

"What are these mysterious meetings about?" I was curious, Kolya wasn't given to secrets.

"I'll tell you when I see you. Will you need to work while I'm in town?" There was the tiniest edge in Kolya's voice and I was pretty certain his past girlfriends had always been willing to put their lives on hold for him.

"I don't think so. There's a party at the Eardisley Gallery, I should go to. And I'd like to go along to the sale at Carlyle's. I'm not bidding, but it's always interesting to hear the latest gossip and see who's buying. But you'll enjoy those, I think. Or I can go on my own, if you don't want to."

"No, no. We'll go together." Kolya's tone was firm, and I suspected this was part of his plan to convince me that we should put our relationship onto a more official footing. I tried to hide my sigh; it was a well-trodden conversational path and one I didn't want to revisit. If we lived on different sides of the Atlantic, how could it be other than how it was?

"That's great. Look, I'm exhausted. Do you mind if I call you back tomorrow?"

"Okay. I need to give the dancers their notes and to start warming up soon for tonight. It takes longer to get my muscles moving these days."

"I'm sorry, I forgot. I hope it goes well." It was the first performance of a new work. I should have been there but I'd had to cancel because of today's jaunt.

"It should do." Kolya was dismissive, the arrogance that came from thirty years as one of the best in the world. Arrogance he was mostly oblivious of. "It's not the most taxing piece I've ever performed. But even so, it would have been nice if you were here."

"I know. It couldn't be helped."

"We need to think of a way of making it easier to be there for each other."

"Maybe," I conceded. But there it was again, the reproach. I didn't need him to be around, to smile and clap and be the loyal and supportive partner, but it seemed he wanted that from me. Or was it just that he was used to that level of devotion?

"Goodnight, my darling. I'll speak to you tomorrow."

"Ring me when you get home and tell me how it went. I don't mind how late." I suspected I'd be awake anyway, peaceful dreams chased away by today's horrors.

Hanging up, I took another mouthful of wine and turned the TV back up, letting my mind switch off again as I watched a light-hearted documentary involving two comedians driving across Mongolia.

My involvement with Kolya was something else I didn't want to think about tonight. I wished I could be completely open with him about my recovery work, make him understand the buzz I got from the challenge of it and the satisfaction when it all came together. But he refused to see that, concentrating on the less salubrious elements, and insisting that I should focus on my consultancy work and thus have more time to spend with him. Kolya had always had everything his own way. Indeed, a team of people looked after him to make sure he was never hindered in the pursuit of his art. Someone saying "no" was new to him and not something he was adapting to easily.

I was dozing on the sofa when the sound of the front door opening jolted me awake. Alert, I leapt to my feet, pulse racing.

"Who's that?" I called, heading for the hallway, skidding to a halt on the polished boards when I saw my neighbour, Flora, standing there, a tin of Whiskas in her hand.

"It's just me. Sorry, I didn't know you were back. You usually text and so I popped down to feed Arthur. He wasn't keen on what I gave him earlier, so I thought I'd see if he liked this tinned stuff." Flora's voice tailed off as she looked at me. "Is everything okay? I'm sorry if I startled you."

"That's all right. I just wasn't expecting anyone and it's been a bit of a tough day. At least I didn't grab the poker." I forced a smile.

"Quite. Shall we have a cup of tea? Or wine?" I could hear the concern in Flora's voice. "And you can tell me what happened today."

And, sympathy and concern weakening my composure, that was when the tears began, just a few that I tried to force back, but as she put an arm round me and guided me back to the sofa, I started weeping, the shock and fear and sadness pouring out of me.

Unable to hold back, the need to talk to someone overwhelming my usual discretion, I told Flora what had happened, details gulped out between sobs as I calmed down again. When I got to the end of the story, Pete's team tight around me with guns in hands, being bundled into the relative safety of the car, I looked up at Flora and saw the shock on her face.

"You saw someone shot?"

"Not exactly." Somehow, it felt important to make that clear. "I saw him slump, saw the woman with the gun walking away. I didn't see her approach him or I would have shouted to warn him. I saw her leaving the scene with the bag of cash I'd given him for the painting."

"Did the police catch her?" Her eyes were wide.

"I don't know. I checked the Cézanne was the real deal and we went to the airport. I imagine the police came."

"But you were witnesses." Flora was one of the most upstanding people I knew.

"Well, yes. But we were also paying a ransom to known criminals, had a painting worth millions, and were carrying weapons of dubious legality. With the best will in the world, we weren't going to hang around for the cops."

There was a silence. I found a tissue in my pocket and blew my nose, wishing I'd had more of a grip on my emotions and hadn't blurted all this out. Flora was a music teacher at a local private school. We'd been good friends ever since I'd moved into the flat below hers but she was a little wary of my sideline in art recovery, sharing with Kolya a wish that I would forego the adrenaline buzz and stick to curating rich people's art collections.

"Who do you think shot him?"

"I don't know. It could have been the people he worked with who wanted to cut him out of his share of the ransom payment. Or, more likely, it was my client wanting both his painting and to keep the cash."

"Really?"

"It's possible." I blew my nose again. "But if it was Navarro, he should have made sure that I knew nothing and saw nothing. It's a small world and I can't afford a rumour to go around that I might have colluded with the shooting. I know it sounds odd, given the people I deal with, but I have to be seen as trustworthy. Plausible deniability and all that."

"I can see that. But you could have been hurt."

"No, not really. I had Pete and three of his guys with me. And a vest, and my own gun. I was safe. But it was a shock. I've never seen anything like that before." Flora said nothing, just gave me another hug, and I struggled to change the subject. "Anyway, how come you're home on a Friday night? Don't you and David the ex-priest normally go out and do couple things?"

"Ah. David and I broke up." Flora smiled, not appearing devastated about this.

"Really? When?"

"Yesterday." She shrugged, dismissively. "No-one needs that much Catholic guilt and angst in their life. And he was a bit of a prick."

"Maybe. I couldn't possibly comment," I said, wanting normal conversation and laughter to push away memories of the day. "Shall I get us more wine?"

After Flora had gone and I'd locked up, I went to bed but couldn't sleep, my mind back to spinning between images of the dead man and his fur-coated assassin. Checking the time, I knew Kolya would be on stage. Maybe I could have made it there if I'd tried, visions of sprinting through JFK airport to get a taxi across town presented themselves as possibilities. If I was committed to our relationship, wouldn't I have made sure I was there? I sent him a text, wishing him luck, but it felt a bit half-hearted.

And I saw that Pete had texted me earlier, asking if I was okay and telling me to call if I needed to talk. I didn't ring him, just sent a brief, reassuring message back. It might have made me feel better, but late-night chats with Pete weren't a good idea. Too easy for the subject to drift to more personal topics and I didn't want to be reminded that I might have made some rash decisions.

At one am, almost as soon as I'd dropped off, my phone buzzed and I fumbled for it. It was a message from Jane Drinkwater, a journalist on a broadsheet newspaper:

"Hi Kate, hope I haven't woken you. I was just looking for a quote about this stolen painting if you've got a minute? Something about who you think the thieves are likely to be, whether you think it's likely to be found, whether it would have been stolen to order. That type of thing. Can you call me when you get this, please? Thanks so much x"

Instantly awake, I tapped the message to call her back. She'd been a useful contact in the past so I probably owed her.

"Hi, it's Kate. What stolen painting?" I hoped I seemed more together and less sleepy than I was.

"Oh, brilliant. I didn't ring in case you'd gone to bed." Jane sounded relieved. "I've got so little info to work with here."

"Tell me about the theft."

"A Mark Rothko painting. Taken from a home in central London a few hours ago. I got a tip from a cop."

"Whose was it?" Alert at the name, my mind was running through the people I could think of who might have a work like that in their homes. With a very conservative value of ten million pounds as an absolute minimum, possibly a lot more, it was a fairly short list.

"Yuri Sokolov. Although that's not official yet. You know him?"

"By reputation mainly." I'd seen him around at auctions, parties, and so on. An oligarch with a shady reputation and usually flanked by minders, he wasn't given to social chit-chat. From what I gathered, he had quite a collection of modern art.

"So what do you think? Some other oligarch had it stolen to hang on his own wall?" Jane was clearly hoping for a more dramatic explanation than I could give her.

"Jane, you know that doesn't happen. Someone will have taken it and they'll possibly ransom it back to him or the insurers. How big was it?"

"Not sure. My contact said it was massive, but he wasn't specific."

"Hmm." I hesitated. Most thieves went for smaller works —easier to carry, to hide, to move. "If it doesn't turn up quickly, it'll probably be used as currency by various criminals until someone decides to return it for the reward. It could take years to resurface."

"Come on, Kate. I need a better quote than that for my readers."

"Okay, you can say that paintings like this can be used as a kind of underworld currency by thieves. And you can say that whoever took it must have been very experienced to get into a house as secure as Sokolov's would have been, so they knew what they were doing. But don't use my name."

"Really?"

"Really. You never know, at some point I might have a professional interest in it." I didn't want my name prematurely attached to this.

"And if you do, you'll talk to me?"

"Maybe."

After I'd hung up, all my instincts tingling, I tapped out another text, this time to Joe Cathcart, insurance underwriter to the super-rich and one of my regular clients:

"Hey, Joe. Is that stolen Rothko yours? Looks intriguing..."

A reply pinged back almost immediately.

"Too fucking right it is. Tied up with the police just now. Can I call you in the morning?"

"Anytime."

"Thanks, babe."

I smiled, glad I'd touted for business just this once. This would be interesting.

3

In its pre-dawn state, Edinburgh was beautiful. Even in the rain with the slick granite cobbles glinting in the streetlights, the symmetry of the Georgian townhouses and the railings around garden squares were calm and serene. The broad streets of the New Town—wide enough to turn a coach and four, so they said, although it tended to be Volvos these days—were empty save for a few early birds like me, dog-walkers and runners nodding a greeting as we splashed past each other.

Running along Princes Street beside the hulk of the castle rock, smooth, silent, passengerless trams overtook me. There were few people, not many cars, no tourists—perfect. Looping round through Comely Bank and into Inverleith just as dawn broke, I cut through the park, nodding again at more dog-walkers and skirting the early morning boot camp attendees who were already doing press-ups on the wet grass.

After six miles, I felt awake despite my restless night. I took a shower and fed Arthur. He looked at me and the offering I made with utter disdain. Not in the mood for his attitude, I tied my wet hair back and headed out to a nearby café. All man-buns and bits of bicycle hanging on the walls it was peak-hipster. Good coffee though, and Wi-Fi.

There was an email waiting for me from the Cézanne's owner, and I smiled rather grimly at his expressions of gratitude and praise. He'd paid my invoice promptly and added a bonus that made me shudder. I'd donate it to charity.

Sotheby's had launched the catalogue for their big Old Masters sale and I forwarded the notification to Jason. We'd discuss it later.

He was my biggest-spending client, a tech billionaire, he'd taken it into his head that he needed some Old Masters to make his newly decorated Palo Alto dining room look 'real classy, you know?' Oh, I knew, I knew. Christmas dinner would always be enhanced by a Tintoretto over the fireplace.

Jason—Silicon Valley via Harvard and Texas—had limited knowledge of art but boundless enthusiasm and gave me a free hand with his money. In return, balancing my knowledge with his developing tastes, we were building a wonderful collection of mainly twentieth-century works that he truly loved.

I was selective in my clients and was doubtful about the Texan tech-bro when he first approached me. But I liked him, brashness and all, and he had a charm that was hard to say no to. He was also quite a philanthropist, quietly funding an educational charity and entire aid convoys to the world's most desperate places. I knew that the art he collected might one day appreciate enough in value to pay for the building of another hospital and so I made sure that I bought well, playing to my reputation as a sharp negotiator.

There was, I noticed with a wave of the relief I always

felt, not an email from Chris, my violent ex-boyfriend, who frequently defied the restraining order that kept him well away from me, and liked to send me messages every month or so with photos taken during our relationship. Nothing I wouldn't want my mother seeing; I'm not foolish enough to let anyone take that sort of picture. There was always a disposable email address behind the messages, usually with just an innocuous line about how great I'd looked or how lovely that day had been.

He'd sent a few more vitriolic ones when he'd first seen me around town with Pete, Edinburgh being a small place, although that was not long after he'd got out of prison and I'd let it pass, assuming that he was still feeling a little sore about his four-month stay at Her Majesty's Pleasure. Now he was back to his old life working in the financial sector and as a stalwart of his former school's ex-pupils rugby club and I had decided to ignore the messages, not giving him the satisfaction of knowing that they got to me.

This morning though, all my attention was on the stolen Rothko. My research revealed little about the work. Bought directly from the artist in the 1950s, it remained in the same family until it was sold two years earlier in a private sale to an anonymous buyer for an unknown sum. The only image I could ferret out online was a blurry reproduction taken from a book about the architect who designed the then-owner's house. Assuming it had been accepted as genuine, it would be in the *Catalogue Raisonee*, the complete survey of Rothko's works, but I would need to go up to the National Library on George IV Bridge for that.

I continued to ferret around the internet and pulled together more information. It seemed the Rothko had been believed lost in a fire that gutted the owner's house in the 1980s. Then it turned up in a storage locker after twenty years or so and was restored. When it went on show in a small gallery, there was a piece in the New York Times arts section titled "Rothko's phoenix rises from the ashes". Then nothing. The gallery owner had been cagey about who they'd been selling it on behalf of, and it seemed they were no longer in business. That the painting had re-emerged having been thought lost was a miracle, that it was now missing again was heartbreaking.

Despite my lack of artistic ability, it was Mark Rothko who, indirectly, encouraged me to follow the career path I did. In London on a school trip, my friends bunked off to Oxford Street to buy clothes, and, geek that I was, I sloped off to an art gallery. There was an exhibition of Rothko's work and I'd sat in front of one for I don't know how long, just absorbed in the depth of colour and its intensity. Rothko said that his work was about life and death, the very essence of human drama, and this painting was overwhelming to a no doubt overly sentimental teenager. Back then, I may not have understood it, but that didn't matter. It moved me.

The man sitting next to me must have seen the emotion on my face and passed me a tissue. Well into his seventies, he had paint-stained fingers and an air of malt whisky and charm. In retrospect, probably not the sort of person teenage girls should fall into conversation with. He asked if I painted and I said no, that art fascinated me but I couldn't draw for toffee. Then my insightful new friend told me that feeling art was as important as being able to create it, because if art didn't move people then it was just so much paint on canvas, devoid of meaning. And that made me realise that loving art, connecting with it on an emotional level, and being able to communicate my knowledge might be enough.

So, back at school, instead of continuing to drive my teachers mad with my indecision about exam choices, I told them that I wanted to go to university to study art history. My art teacher, knowing my ham-fisted attempts with pencil and paint, raised an eyebrow, but tutored me all the same and was both pleased and surprised when I got an A and headed off to art school.

Consequently, whenever I travelled to a city with a gallery that housed one of Rothko's paintings that was new to me, I'd always make a trip to find it and to say a silent thank you to him and the careers-advice-dispensing, twinkling-eyed stranger, who pointed my life in the right direction.

Jason wanted to buy a Rothko because he liked the size of the canvases and thought one would be striking in his house. I was determined to find him a work that would rock him back on his heels, to show him that these paintings weren't just over-sized blocks of colour but raw emotion. And when I found the right one, I would finally accept his invitation to visit his Bay Area mansion and ask if I could simply sit alone with the painting for a while, drinking in its power and scale.

That one of these amazing works was missing, possibly lost forever, saddened me and I fidgeted while I waited for Joe to call, waiting to get started on finding it.

Joe rang after lunch. An Essex boy in bespoke Savile Row, he was permanently stressed, paid my not-insubstantial invoices on the nail, and had a straightforward, if rather sweary, manner that I liked.

"Hi, Joe. Nice to hear from you."

"Is it, Kate? Is it really? I tell you, my life is hell today. Utter fucking hell. You don't understand what a disaster this bloody Rothko theft is."

"Go on." I leaned back in my desk chair, doodling on a pad of paper.

"I have a client who expects his insurers to pay out without question and is threatening everything from litigation to knee-capping if we try to get out of it. But what am I supposed to do? They got in through an unsecured skylight. What does he expect from me? That I just say 'never mind' and hand over a cheque for ten million? For fuck's sake." He paused, and I heard him take a slurp of something, probably the strong black coffee he consumed so much of.

"I can see why Sokolov's upset." I tried to sound soothing. There was no point in anything more until Joe had finished venting.

"How do you know it was his?"

"A little bird told me. It was a beautiful painting."

"Was it? I don't care if it was the bloody Hay Wain on a table mat. I just need to find the damn thing."

"I can imagine. I might be able to help. Your investigators not feeling confident?"

"Don't take the piss, Kate." Another slurp of coffee. How Joe slept at night, I had no idea. "You know fine that my boys have to stick to rules you bloody well ignore when it suits you. That's why we subcontract to you and why you charge us an arm and a leg."

"You come to me because I get results." I didn't like the insinuation that I exploited his misfortune.

"Yes, well, I'm sorry." He sounded contrite. "I'm still hoping that the thieves realise it's too hot to keep and just ask for a ransom. Mind you, fuck knows what state it's in.

They didn't so much cut it from the wooden stretchers as hack it from them."

"No suspects?" I asked. It would be a starting point.

"Not really."

"So what do you want me to do?"

"Short of producing it like a rabbit from a fucking hat? Ask questions, see what the gossip is. People tell my guys nothing, but they all talk to you." More coffee. "I don't know how you do that."

"I think it's because I'm not an ex-cop like your investigators. And the dealers and auction houses want to keep in with me."

"Okay, what do you need?"

"Hi-res image of the painting, CCTV footage, witness statements, anything else you can think of. Where was Sokolov when it was taken? And his housekeeper and security people for that matter? I'll need to see the crime scene, too."

"Sokolov won't like that. You should have seen how twitchy he was when the police were there."

"He wants his insurance money. Or his painting. And he probably needs my help. He'll have to put up with it." I shrugged; placating Yuri Sokolov was Joe's problem, not mine.

"I'll talk to him. But he's Russian and you know how these oligarchs can be tricky."

"I'm well aware of that."

"When can you be here?"

"Tomorrow? I'm planning a few days in town with my own tricky Russian."

"How convenient for us both." I could hear the smile in Joe's voice.

"I'm not sure Kolya will see it like that. He was hoping

we'd have a peaceful work-free break. But if I get an early flight I can be at your office by eleven. We'll take a look then. And try to relax, Joe."

"Fat chance."

Already feeling the fizz of interest that comes with a new job, I checked my email and found the information I needed from Joe. Opening the CCTV footage, I watched a figure in black, with a balaclava hiding their face, appear down a flight of stairs onto a spacious and grand landing. The only furniture I could see was a chest of drawers, but the artwork on the walls was stunning, despite the grainy quality. A small Picasso, one of Matisse's graphic dancing figures, a Miro, and more that I couldn't quite make out—all highly covetable.

And there was the Rothko. The figure headed straight for it, not even glancing at the millions of pounds' worth of art on the other walls. I caught my breath and winced as I saw the thief root in a pocket for a knife and then slit the canvas from its frame. Then, he rolled it up after a fashion—no easy task—secured it with a cord of some sort, and ran back up the stairs carrying it awkwardly.

I made a coffee and watched the footage again and again. Several things intrigued me, starting with the question of why that painting in the first place. It wasn't the most portable item and thieves don't usually make life harder for themselves than they need to. Sure, that little Joan Miró wasn't worth as much but they weren't stealing for retail and in terms of a reward, it might be just as profitable. The Rothko was huge, about the same height as the thief. Even cut from the wooden stretchers that gave structure to the cotton of the canvas, with a dozen or more layers of paint and glazes, it was cumbersome. And then the thief escaped across the roof, this enormous painting rolled up like a carpet under their arm.

Even if you were sure-footed and didn't mind heights, that was a lot of trouble to go to. A job like this took planning and the thief would have known what other works were likely to be in the property even if they didn't know the details. A pro would have taken something easier to carry and then to hide. But this was too slick a job to be the work of an amateur.

No, this thief came for the Rothko. And they knew that skylight would be unsecured. No opportunist would be hanging around on the roof hoping to get lucky. I texted Joe:

"I'd also like background reports on Sokolov's domestic and security staff. Someone left that window unlocked. And why wasn't the alarm on?"

I smiled to myself, anticipating the challenge of outsmarting that thief, pitting my guile and cunning against theirs. Although art recovery, with its stakeouts in deserted warehouses and endless frustrating dead-ends was less glamorous than my consultancy work, it was the side of my life that gave me the excitement I needed.

Sometimes I was hired to recover artworks looted during World War Two, which was satisfying, but most of my work was looking for art taken in more conventional ways. Those paintings might be stolen and held to ransom, like the Cézanne, or they would be taken to use as collateral in drug or arms deals. Sometimes they were taken by petty criminals simply because the opportunity presented itself. An artwork could make its way through several criminal hands before finally being handed over to me in an underground car park or a train station.

Hardly ever, no, forget that, absolutely never, were paintings taken by eccentric billionaires with dubious morals and impeccable taste to adorn the walls of secret galleries in their Bond villain-style lairs. A pity, those pictures would probably have been easier to track down because according to films, that sort of person liked to brag and my recovery work would involve more cocktail dresses and stilettos, and less need for thermals while hanging around snowy parks and the like.

People used my skills rather than relying on the police for many reasons. The money that paid for the painting might not have been squeaky-clean or maybe galleries didn't want word to spread that their security hadn't been all it could be, or perhaps the owner wanted someone less restricted by the rules other agencies had to follow. Besides, even if they knew where to start looking, the local plod would be extremely unlikely to hop on a private plane to St Petersburg to pay a six-figure ransom in used fifty-dollar bills if that was what was needed.

Not that anyone called it a ransom. Officially, it was referred to as "paying a reward for information leading to the return of stolen property" to stay on the right side of the Proceeds of Crime Act. That was in the UK. Overseas, and where works had travelled through many hands and many jurisdictions, things were more flexible.

My job was to track the pieces through a labyrinth of dubious contacts, sharp-eared dealers and helpful branches of international law enforcement, find the thieves, drug cartel or criminal gang in possession of the artwork, and negotiate for its return.

Sometimes recovering a piece took a day or two, a

mobile phone number and a clip of CCTV footage. At other times, art seemed to disappear like mist on a summer's morning, clues vanishing as I reached out to snatch at them, and it would take a long time before those ephemeral fragments became hard facts. But for the people looking for their looted Leibermanns or their stolen Chagalls, I was just the person they needed.

4

A couple of days later, while I was in the taxi on the way from the airport, Kolya rang, his face flashing up on my phone. He'd arrived in London the night before and was already ensconced at the Belgravia hotel he'd booked for our stay.

"Hello, you," I said, smiling at his rumpled hair and reading glasses.

"Good morning. I'm calling to tell you I'm tired and grumpy and my jet-lag means I can't sleep. Even in this lovely suite. I wish you were here." He grinned, blue eyes twinkling.

"Really? If you're grumpy I'm not sure I want to be there."

"I'm more cheerful when I'm with you. Even Marcella has commented on it."

"Goodness." That surprised me. Marcella was one of Kolya's assistants, so Parisian she was almost a caricature. She utterly terrified me.

"When will you get to the hotel this afternoon?"

"Don't know. I'll drop my case off, then go to Joe's place

and on to see the crime scene. I thought I might call in at Helen's gallery after that as I haven't seen her for a while. What time is your meeting?"

"Two. So you're coming to the hotel now?" His face lit up.

"Only to leave my case. I'm already cutting it fine. If you go down to the foyer in about ten minutes, I'll have time for a quick hug, but that's it. I'm sorry."

"It's fine." I saw the tiniest flash of annoyance in his eyes. "I'm still in bed. I'll see you when I get back from my meeting."

"Are you going to tell me what that's about? You've been very mysterious."

"No. But I will afterwards."

"I'll look forward to it." I smiled. "And I'll be back by four or five at the very latest."

"I shouldn't be long after that. Shall we go out for dinner?"

"How about room service? I've been up since four and you're jet-lagged. How about a cosy evening in? I just want to spend time catching up with you." The thought of dashing around town all day and then having to get dressed up to go to the sort of place Kolya liked, didn't fill me with enthusiasm.

"As you wish."

"I'd better go, darling. We're nearly there. See you later."

The taxi stopped outside the row of Belgravia town-houses converted into the very exclusive Chippenham Hotel where Kolya liked to stay when he was in town and I jumped out with my case, almost immediately relinquishing it to a uniformed doorman who dashed forward to relieve me of it.

A little disappointed that Kolya hadn't thrown on some

clothes and nipped down to give me a quick kiss, I got back in the cab and directed the driver to Joe's office, focusing myself on being an efficient, capable professional, rather than a slightly miffed girlfriend.

I thought back to the first time I'd met Kolya. It was at a gallery party in New York and I had no idea who he was as he walked towards me. Even when we were introduced his name didn't ring any bells, but looking at the swivelling heads of the ladies-who-lunch, they were all very aware of exactly who Nikolai Ivanovich was. We talked about the art on show that night, he asked what I did and then asked if I would look at his collection and advise on how to make it more coherent. He'd had to sell some prized pieces when he divorced and felt it was a good time to refresh things.

Men inviting me to look at their etchings is not a euphemism in my business, and the next day I visited his home to see his current artworks. He'd just moved from his brownstone in Brooklyn to a warehouse downtown that he'd converted, keeping the top floor's mostly open-plan 5,000-odd square foot and its roof terraces for himself.

"I didn't realise dancing paid so well." I'd laughed, instinctively calculating the budget his art advisor would have to work with.

"It doesn't." He'd smiled back as he opened a bottle of champagne. "But when I was a child in the Soviet Union we couldn't own property and when I moved to the States, it was important to always have a home to call my own. Security too; dancers are only one bad fall away from unemployment. So I bought houses and fixed them up and kept some of them. I've moved to contemporary dance and I choreograph these days but when I still danced classical ballet, I was one of the best-paid dancers in the world. Despite that, I've made my money with property." He had left the chaos of post-Communist Russia when he was twenty, and never returned, claiming that America, where he'd now lived for almost thirty years, was home.

Over time, we'd got to know one another, and although he invited me to dinner frequently and made it clear—albeit in a very gentlemanly manner—that he was attracted to me, I kept things on a business footing. Not least because I was still involved with Pete, to begin with at any rate. Then one spring evening, a couple of months after I'd ended things with Pete, Kolya cooked me dinner in his Tribeca loft and everything changed.

Six months on, I knew that we were at a turning point in our relationship. Chris's violence had left me with a persistent fear of commitment. Rarely in the same place for more than a couple of weeks, my involvement with Pete was fine because neither of us could offer more. I'd ended things when I realised that without major life changes for one or both of us, there was no real future for us beyond that which we currently enjoyed. I felt it was time to grow up and dip a toe in the waters of a "proper" relationship, whatever that was.

And now that I'd tried that, I needed to decide if it was really what I wanted and if I was prepared to make the necessary compromises that a long-term future with Koyla would require. He wanted me to make changes in my life because he was tied to New York for work purposes. And if I wasn't willing to do that, then I knew I should walk away, that this was another relationship with no future.

It had to be said that life was much simpler when I only had to worry about gangs of organised criminals, finding beautiful paintings for clients such as Jason, and conducting a part-time and hassle-free affair with Pete.

Joe Cathcart's office was in an expensive part of town, just like his clients. And the part they saw was very slick; glass-walled conference rooms, some good art on the walls, and designer Italian sofas. I said hello to Debbie, his receptionist, and she buzzed me through to the back office which had a very different feel with desks piled high with files.

Despite the fancy tailoring that Joe preferred now that he was middle-aged and successful, he was an Essex boy through and through. I liked him a lot and I would always take a job for him if he asked. That, and he had recently put me on a retainer so that he knew he had first call on my skills. I smiled my appreciation as Debbie handed me a coffee and turned as Joe emerged from his office.

Today, he looked all out of his usual charm and energy. He seemed especially stressed, running his hands through his dark hair. I made to kiss his cheek as usual and he practically shrugged me off.

"It's good to see you, Joe."

"I wish I could say it was good to see you too, love. But you being here means that everything is a fucking nightmare. Come on through."

I followed him to his office and sat down while he poured another mug of coffee. I wondered if caffeine was a good idea. Perhaps whisky or Valium would be better.

"Sokolov not calmed down then?"

"Not a chance. He's threatening all sorts and now I've got his lawyers getting stroppy. We're not bloody Direct Line. It's not as though he's pranged his motor in the supermarket car park. We don't pay out 48 hours later and send a courtesy Monet to fill the gap on the sodding wall."

I smiled, despite myself, but I saw his point. His client would not be a tolerant man. I was well-used to that; my clients were often impatient, but Sokolov's frustration would not be so good-natured. I'd done some research into his background and knew that you didn't get to be as rich as him in post-Communist Russia without being ruthless.

"I'll do what I can."

"Thank you." Joe took a slurp of coffee while I took my laptop from my bag, moving my chair next to his while it booted up.

"Look." I pulled up the CCTV film and hit play. "You see how the thief appears at the bottom of the stairs and runs along the landing?" He nodded. "Look at the other paintings. All desirable, all infinitely more portable, save for the Matisse, and just as valuable on the black market. Possibly more so. Much easier to hide, for sure. It makes no sense to take the Rothko."

"Stolen to order?" Joe sounded more hopeful than realistic. It would be a clue at least.

"Not in the way you mean, but they were definitely after that particular painting." I ran the footage again, and we watched the black-clad figure run down the landing—tall, slim, agile. "And look how he cuts it from the stretchers. A professional stealing to order would be more careful."

"You'd think."

"What have the police said?" The Met's Art and Antiques Squad numbered a handful of cops these days and I didn't expect them to have many resources to contribute to this case.

"Not a lot. They seem to be looking at it as just another

burglary, albeit a high-value one. They're expecting a ransom demand."

"I'm not." I folded my laptop back up and slid it into my well-used Mulberry Bayswater.

"No?"

"They came specifically for that painting. He doesn't even glance at the others, just heads for the Rothko. If he wants to make a quick buck, the little Picasso would be a much better option. You could fit that in a backpack, frame and all."

"So now what?" Joe drained his coffee cup.

"Now, we take a look ourselves. What's the story with the housekeeper and where was Sokolov on the night it was taken?" This was one of the things that I'd been curious about; just how had the thief managed to get past all the personnel and security that went with a house like that?

"He was in Berlin apparently, most of his security people were with him. The one left behind seems to have been asleep or something. Wasn't watching the bloody CCTV, at any rate. Housekeeper was in her quarters and also claims to have been asleep. She says she heard nothing. Both of them claim not to have noticed the skylight was unlatched." Joe shrugged and I got the impression he was doubtful of both their stories.

"Have the cops got any suspects?"

"They're not saying much, Sokolov being a celebrity and all that. And litigious. They suggested Lucien de Bruin, but I think that's because his was the only name they could come up with."

"I can see why they'd think that. The rooftop aspect is his style, but he'd be more careful with the canvas for a start. He might be a thief—and remember no-one's ever pinned anything on him – but he'd do a better job than that."

"Nor are the boys in blue best pleased that I was more interested in what you had to say than their conclusions. All the same, I think they're hoping you'll think of a few more suspects."

"Are they now?" I grinned. "But I work for you, not them."

"Exactly." Joe smiled wryly, aware that the police clumsily chasing this painting would just get in the way and might mean it never resurfaced. Which would be far more expensive for him than any ransom I might negotiate. He looked at me, assessing.

"You okay, though? Pete told me what happened in St Petersburg."

"I'm fine." I didn't need to tell him about the images of the dead man falling from the bench that still flashed into my mind now and then. "Pete needn't be concerned."

"He's just protective of you."

I looked at Joe over the rim of my mug, a warning in my eyes he didn't spot. But Joe's wife was Pete's cousin and to Joe, that made me practically family. Normal social boundaries didn't exist.

"He's no need to be."

"You know Pete. That's how he is. You meant a lot to him. Still do, for that matter."

"You reckon?" Pete and I didn't talk about feelings. Never had. Maybe we should have.

"I don't understand why you two split up. For all those protestations about not wanting a committed relationship, you were better together than a lot of married couples I know." Joe gave me a sharp look.

"It's complicated." I sighed and stood up, wanting to change the subject and get on. I'd moved on from Pete because it was the sensible thing to do. And Kolya was the perfect partner, in many ways. “Shall we go?”

“We’d better. Our friend Yuri is surprisingly keen on punctuality for someone who feels entitled to keep everyone else waiting.”

As I pulled my coat back on, Debbie appeared. Smiling apologetically, she informed Joe that a detective chief inspector was on the phone for him. He rolled his eyes and looked at me, weighing his options.

“Fuck. This might take a while.”

“I could go on ahead? You could catch me up?”

“Okay.” Joe looked doubtful and scribbled a Chelsea address on a sticky note. “But be diplomatic.”

“Of course. I’ll be my most utterly charming self.” I smiled, took the post-it, and headed for the door.

Stepping out into the street, hailing a cab, I grinned and felt the buzz I always did at this point, the moment where I got to put myself in the thief’s head and work out exactly how they’d carried out the heist. Indeed, how I would have done it.

5

Sokolov's house, on a busy street and flanked by similar properties, was anonymous and private and unfriendly. High walls, tall, precisely trimmed hedges behind them and who knew what behind those. At the dark grey gate, I pressed the buzzer, looked up as I heard a camera whirring to take a look at me, and announced myself to the disembodied voice that demanded my name. No-one replied, but a lock clicked and when I pushed open the gate, I found myself face to face with an enormous security guard in a cheap suit and with a too-short haircut.

"Morning, I'm Kate Carpenter. I think you're expecting me." I smiled, just as I'd promised Joe I would, but he didn't reciprocate.

"Come with me, Miss Carpenter." His voice was heavily accented; Russia or somewhere around there, and I followed him through the front door. The hallway was decorated in harmonious tones of beige. The furniture was bland, the carpets thick, and the artwork good, if somewhat second division for someone of Sokolov's wealth, save for an exquisite Giacometti bronze figure on a side table. Nonetheless, it all reeked of money. The man-mountain held out a form.

"You need to sign this Non-Disclosure Agreement. And you can leave your phone here."

I raised an eyebrow; usually, a personal assistant or secretary would appear to deal with paperwork. Perhaps people were happier to sign whatever they were told to if ordered to by an intimidating security guard.

"I don't think so." I handed the form back. "I'm here to find the painting that was stolen on your watch. Just tell your boss I'm here and let's get on with it."

He gave me a filthy look—maybe the crack about the less than adequate security was too close to the bone—and left me in the hall. I pulled my offending phone from the pocket of my jeans and texted Joe:

"They're not exactly welcoming. Will you be long?"

A door opened and a woman appeared. Pulling on a coat as she hurried towards the door, almost shoving me aside, she wore a denim miniskirt and a thin t-shirt. There was a livid bruise on her cheek barely hidden by her bleached blonde hair. She was unhappy and unexpected in such an elegant, expensive setting. I stepped towards her, an automatic impulse to ask if she was okay on my lips. Our eyes met, but before she could speak, a man appeared from the doorway behind her and she flinched as she turned and saw him.

Like the guard who'd let me in, this man was dressed in a bargain basement suit and cheap shoes. Another security employee of some sort. He glanced at me with cold eyes but didn't speak. Grabbing the young woman by the arm, not giving her a chance to struggle or say anything, he shoved her back through the door she'd come out of. It slammed shut, and I heard angry words. It was the briefest of interactions, just a few seconds, but it unsettled me, bringing back memories of the fear I'd once felt in my relationship with Chris.

"Please come with me." The heavy who'd admitted me reappeared and led the way through to a library, cutting off my thoughts about the bruised woman and bringing me back to the present. I wanted to know if she was okay, but for the moment I needed to concentrate on this. I'd ask later. "Mr Sokolov will be with you shortly." He left me and my phone buzzed. Joe:

"Two minutes away in a cab. Be nice."

I sighed. But if being nice right now would smooth the way and even help reduce Joe's stress levels, then I'd do it. I liked Joe. I'd feel bad if he had a heart attack and he'd looked alarmingly close to it earlier.

Left on my own, I looked around the library. It was more interesting than the hall, with lots of very tidy bookshelves and an Andy Warhol portrait of Marilyn Monroe between the tall French windows. Leaning against the heavily carved and gilded desk—an incongruous example of dictator chic—I tried to look patient and professional for the CCTV camera I knew would be watching.

Sokolov's background was murky. He grew up and began his career in Russia just as Communism ended and seemingly rose without a trace, from the child of factory workers to an incomprehensibly vast fortune in less than two decades. My internet browsing meant that I knew he divided his time between homes all over the world and the biggest and tackiest yacht imaginable. No-one seemed to know exactly what his business interests were but oil, gas, import-export, and commodities were mentioned. The sort of vague things that always sounded as though they were a front for something.

They must have been substantial holdings though, as from what I could gather the Rothko was far from being the priciest piece in his collection. Allegedly. He seemed to buy mostly in private sales rather than publicly at auction, so pinning down specific paintings and prices was nigh on impossible. I knew him by sight; we went to the same parties and auctions, but we'd never spoken or been introduced. Nor did he seem the kind of man you'd casually strike up a conversation with, even assuming there wasn't always a minder between him and the rest of the world.

The door opened and Yuri Sokolov entered, not looking pleased to see me leaning against the desk. About six feet tall, with unconvincingly dark brown hair and expressionless grey eyes, he wore dad jeans, loafers and a grey sweatshirt. So much money, so little style. He smiled, not exactly warmly, and held out his hand.

"Miss Carpenter. Yuri Sokolov. Thank you so much for coming."

"How do you do, Yuri?" I shook his hand. He had quite the grip; wanting to show how macho he was, how powerful, how I should be intimidated. I didn't give any indication that I'd even noticed. I wanted to ask about the woman in the hall, but caution warned me to shelve that for the moment. "Please call me Kate. It's quicker and I never see the point of unnecessary formality." I smiled my very nicest smile.

He looked uncomfortable and I got the impression that he very much preferred to be called Mr Sokolov. It's always interesting to see how people respond to the use of their first names. I've noticed that the people who prefer to maintain those barriers are usually the least secure in themselves or they're the people with something to hide. And calling them by their first name throws them off-balance, which can be very revealing.

There was a knock at the door and Joe was ushered in looking just as stressed as when I'd left his office. But no more so, which was positive, I guessed. He flicked a glance at me, assessing the temperature of the room, and I showed him my most charming smile too.

"Mr Sokolov, thank you for being available this morning." Joe was almost obsequious and I rolled my eyes, cutting him off before he started on a long explanation as to who I was and what I do.

"I was just about to explain to Yuri that the first thing I need to see is where the picture was hanging, check out how the thieves gained entry, and then have a look at the frame and anything else that was left behind." I stressed my use of Sokolov's first name just a little.

"You really need to see all that? I have photographs for you to look at." Sokolov was telling me, not really asking a question. "Other people have already examined those things."

"With respect, Yuri, those people weren't me. And other people sometimes miss things. Now, lead the way, please." My smile was getting tired.

The next half an hour or so was interesting. The painting had been hanging on the first-floor landing. The stretchers and the simple wooden frame were still there, the space in the middle a gaping sadness. Around the edges, small fragments of canvas remained, tiny flags of colour that only hinted at what the whole had been.

I squinted and crouched and walked the route from the top floor attic window where the thief had gained entry, down the two flights of stairs to the Rothko. I jumped up to grab the edges of the skylight and pulled myself up to look at the roof, the burn in my shoulder muscles and biceps reminding me to get back to the gym. Whoever had taken the painting had either been pretty fit or had a co-conspirator waiting up on the roof.

I looked at the other artworks that the intruder had passed between entry and target. As I'd thought before, most were more portable and probably more useful to a thief. Despite its size, I took the empty frame off the wall to check the reverse for clues.

Sokolov, flanked by two minders even in his own house, watched my every move, interrupting frequently to point out that someone had already done what I was doing. I kept smiling and took no notice. After a bit, I turned to Joe who looked edgy as he kept reassuring Sokolov that I knew my stuff.

"Joe, you've got DNA swabs and so on?"

"Absolutely. And fingerprints, such as there were. And we've been over everything with a black light. I have all that back at the office for you."

"Good. Can you just come with me for a minute? I want to check those stairs again." I led the way up a flight, and, after making sure that we were out of sight, I lowered my voice. "Get him away from here for a few minutes. The goons, too. I need to be alone with what's left of the painting."

"What?" He looked horrified. "Why?"

"You don't want to know. Just do it." I left him at the top of the stairs while I went part of the way down and pretended to be studying a direction of movement. Then I walked back down the hall to the painting's remnants. It was heart-breaking. I stood staring at the savage hole as though deep in thought and heard Joe suggest that they went back to the library as he had some papers to be signed. I turned around and flashed that winning smile again.

"You carry on. I just need to check a couple of other things but I'll be finished in a few minutes." Sokolov didn't look happy but dutifully led the way downstairs, minders behind him.

I didn't have time to waste. I'd already checked out the angles on the security cameras and knew that if I was close to the frame then my hands would be shielded by my body. Even assuming the cameras were off now, I wasn't going to risk it.

In my bag, I kept a tiny toolkit containing a tape measure, tweezers, pliers, lock picks and so on. Fiddling with it while kneeling in front of the picture as though measuring, no-one watching would have seen me slip a scalpel blade between two fingers. I got closer, as though squinting at some detail, and those same watchers wouldn't have been able to see the strip of canvas that I sliced off with one swift movement, rolling it in my palm, invisible to watching eyes or cameras. I sat back on my heels, giving a final appraising look, and then folded up my toolkit and popped it in my bag.

Making sure that the cameras saw me looking thoughtful and professional, hiding the fact that I wanted to skip downstairs, I followed in the footsteps of Joe and Sokolov. I certainly wasn't going to make our friend Yuri's day, but I was pretty certain I'd saved Joe at least ten million pounds.

6

"So what the fuck was all that about?" Joe and I took a table towards the rear of the café around the corner from Sokolov's place. "You were checking out all kinds of crazy stuff. And what was that business at the end?" I ordered an Americano and rummaged in my bag.

"Shush. 'All that' was me saving you a fortune, my friend." I opened my toolkit and laid the piece of canvas on the table in front of him. Joe looked horrified.

"What have you done? Is this part of that bloody Rothko? Someone has stolen most of it and you're hacking bits off what's left?"

"What do you see, Joe?" I asked, patiently.

"I see that you've lost your fucking mind. Sokolov will go mental over this."

"Sokolov won't know." I pushed the canvas closer to him. "Do you want to know what I see when I look at this?"

"Go on then. It better be good." He took a gulp of coffee and waited, unimpressed.

"You know how artists prime a canvas before they begin work and paint in a plain background?"

"Not really, but if you say so."

"Well, there's a white background to this painting and Rothko didn't paint like that at the time this work supposedly dates from."

"It's a fake?" He looked sceptical. "You're sure?"

"I don't know for certain." I shook my head. "But I've been reading up on the stolen painting and I knew what to look for. There was a similar racket going on in New York a few years ago. You'll need to get it checked by experts and they can look at the pigments and glazes and so on, but I thought taking a piece to examine before Sokolov gets wind and disposes of what's left might be a good idea."

"Fuck," Joe breathed, looking at the fragment of canvas.

"And if I'm right, this leaves three interesting questions for our friend Yuri." I leaned back and sipped my coffee before counting them off on my fingers. "One, did he think it was genuine? Two, did he know that it was a fake from the start and think no-one would ever find out? Or three, did he buy it in good faith, find out it was dodgy, and arrange the theft hoping the insurance policy would settle his claim and no-one would ever know? But whichever is the case, if it's a fake you can just shrug and walk away, surely?'

"But it has provenance. Experts, reports and so on. After it turned up in that storage locker it was assessed and accepted as genuine."

"That can be faked. Criminals have got into archives in the past to insert information to back up their claims and ensure a painting is accepted. People have been fooled plenty of times." I shrugged.

"I sent you copies of the paperwork for this painting."

"You did. And when you pick it apart it's a bit sketchy. It

was bought directly from the artist, so no gallery or dealer records. Not so much as a receipt. Then after its miraculous rediscovery, it's sold privately to Sokolov on behalf of people who want to remain anonymous. All feels rather convenient, don't you think?"

"And the burglary?"

"An open window? Really?" I shook my head. "No-one worth that sort of money leaves a window open at night. It's a set-up. Maybe one of his staff took a bribe to leave the window unlatched? It's intended to look like a professional job but no pro would take that painting. There was a reason they took the Rothko and I suspect it's the third option—Sokolov thought he could recoup his money by claiming on his insurance."

"I'll need to get this looked at by an expert. Check the paint and so on." Joe still didn't sound pleased. I took scissors from my toolkit and snipped the canvas in half, ignoring more wincing. I kept one piece and handed Joe the other.

"There you go."

Joe folded it into his notebook and snapped the elastic round it. I almost regretted making his life more complicated. For all that spotting the forgery would save his business a fortune, I didn't envy him having to tell Sokolov that either he'd been conned or the scam he'd tried to pull had been spotted. When we'd left the house, Sokolov's expression had been carefully blank but there was a hostility in his eyes that chilled me. I didn't envy Joe having to tell him he wouldn't be getting his insurance payout.

"He'll be a nightmare if you're right."

"Well, yes. I think you need to brace yourself for that, Joe. I'll assume it's a theft until you confirm otherwise. I'll make a few calls and so on. You'll let me know if there's a ransom demand?"

"Definitely. That would be simpler." Joe sounded weary.

"Simpler, but not as much fun as outsmarting the bad guys." I grinned broadly. "Cheer up, Joe. Think of the money I've saved you."

Helen Wightman's gallery was a few streets away. It was, like its owner, effortlessly elegant and polished, with pale floors and walls immaculately painted in just the right shade to show off the artworks she had such a good eye for. Walking in, I was immediately drawn to a small Degas sculpture, and then distracted by a series of Matisse cut-outs from the Jazz portfolio.

"Kate, darling. This is an unexpected delight." I swung round as I heard Helen's caramel tones and hugged her. Statuesque at six-two in her stilettos and immaculately tailored Balmain, with her expensively highlighted blonde hair rippling over her shoulders, I felt, as always when I met her, slightly scruffy. And amused. We'd met on our first day at art college when she'd been a black-haired goth in Doc Martens.

"I was in town for a meeting with Joe and had a couple of hours to spare so thought I'd drop in and see if you were free for lunch."

"How lovely."

"But only if you're not busy. I didn't know how long my meeting would take or I'd have called."

"Darling, it's been deathly quiet this morning. Lunch and a glass of champagne with you will cheer me up no end." Helen turned to her assistant, part-Sloane with a non-ironic velvet headband, part identikit gallery girl in a flippy skirt. "Poppy, I'll be out for an hour or two while I attempt to sell Kate some vastly expensive artworks for her clients."

Poppy smiled, flashing lots of upmarket dentistry, and we left, walking towards Jermyn Street in search of lunch.

"You could possibly sell me those cut-outs," I said, thinking of Jason who would love them.

"I'd be delighted to. But you're not really in town today on behalf of your clients, are you?" Helen raised one elegant eyebrow in my direction as we threaded our way between bumper-to-bumper black cabs and shiny sports cars.

"You guess correctly. Let's find somewhere quiet though if we're going to talk about that."

I steered her into a small French restaurant and asked for a table at the back rather than taking the window seat the maître d' had first suggested. That way every art dealer who walked past wouldn't wonder what we were talking about.

"I imagine you were meeting Joe to discuss Yuri Sokolov's stolen Rothko?" Helen glanced at the menu and laid it to one side.

"I was. Have you had any dealings with Sokolov? I only know him by sight."

"He's been in the gallery two or three times but never bought anything. He buys very little on the open market as far as I can tell, but I gather his collection is extensive, so there must be someone fixing things behind the scenes." Helen ordered champagne and sea bass and I nodded, happy to have the same. "Sokolov's girlfriend is described as an art consultant but no-one ever seems to be able to name any of her clients and I don't think anyone's ever heard her speak, so I can't tell you much about her."

"What does his girlfriend look like?" I asked, a recollection of the bruised woman in Sokolov's hallway leaping to mind although with her cheap clothes and ratty hair, I was pretty sure they weren't the same person. So who was she then? Had one of the minders been trying to smuggle his girlfriend out of the house discreetly and she'd strayed into the visitors' area?

"Tall, slim, blonde, well-dressed, amazing cheekbones. But nothing especially distinctive, if you know what I mean. I think she used to be a model, but then, didn't they all?" Helen shrugged, waving an elegant hand dismissively.

"Don't be bitchy. Have you heard anything about dodgy provenance, shady deals, that type of thing?"

"Well," Helen paused while the waiter brought glasses and bread. "Nothing specific, but as you know, buying work that isn't known to the market means it's easier to get ripped off. Look at the sale at Carlyle's later this week. I'm not saying that any of those works are doubtful, but they've been scrutinised pretty carefully by a lot of people and you and I would both be surprised if any weren't legitimate." She looked at me sharply. "You think the Rothko is dubious?"

"I can't possibly comment on that." My refusal told her everything.

"That's interesting because I had heard he was thinking of selling the Rothko. I was going to let you know as you'd said you were after one. Maybe he was selling it on because he knew it was a fake?"

"That crossed my mind, too. It would explain why he was twitchy about me looking too closely at it." I slathered butter on some bread. "And if he was going to sell it privately, it wouldn't be scrutinised as closely as if it went through one of the auction houses."

"Exactly. Offer it privately, price it low enough that the buyer thinks they're getting a good deal and lots of people would go for it. I'll ask around and see if anyone knows what he was planning."

"Great. But be discreet." Gossip was the oil that kept the art world moving, and Helen always knew the latest. It was one of the things that made her such a useful friend. For the moment though, I needed it to be one-way traffic.

"You know I'm discreet when the need arises." Helen paused for a few seconds while the waiter brought our plates and then changed the subject, Sokolov's art collection of less interest than my love-life.

"So tell me about the gorgeous Kolya. Still going well?"

"It's fine, thanks. He's in town at the moment, actually. We'll be at the Eardisley party tomorrow. Will you be there?"

"I think so. Especially if I'll get to see Kolya. Tell me, does he look as incredible naked as my imagination likes to think he does?"

"You're dreadful." I laughed. "I'm not telling you."

"So it's a yes, then? You lucky girl." Then, more seriously, "And does he make you happy?"

"Yes. He does. Things are pretty good on the whole. Weird, though. You know I don't really do proper relationships. I think he'd prefer to progress things faster than I feel comfortable with. But it'll be fine. I'm sure it will."

"I'm glad you're trying out the notion of commitment, though. You might find you enjoy it."

Strolling through Green Park, among ambling tourists and hurrying locals, enjoying the crispness of the autumn air, I checked my phone for messages, my eyebrows lifting at one that seemed altogether too much of a coincidence.

"This is Lucien de Bruin. I need to speak to you."

Lucien de Bruin was an interesting figure in the art world. Ostensibly, he was an art dealer and expert on looted art. It was also suspected—although he'd never been charged, never mind convicted—that he was also a thief. Part of me thought this was a rumour he didn't try hard enough to quash, because he liked the roguish air it gave him, but I also thought it might well be true. Still, if he kept his illicit activities to liberating the odd looted artwork when lawyers and appeals to people's better natures hadn't worked, then it was of no concern to me. Mind you, we'd never come up against each other professionally—the gloves would be off if that happened.

But if he was going to ring me without leaving a number he'd be waiting a long time for a reply. As I thought about this, another call arrived, also from a withheld number.

"Hi. It's Kate. How can I help?"

"Hi. It's Lucien. I need to see you." His voice was urgent, his usual charm nowhere to be seen.

"Where are you?" I asked. De Bruin lived—to the best of my knowledge—on a houseboat in Amsterdam.

"London."

"Me too."

"I know." I spun round, how did he know? Where was he? "I saw you at Sokolov's house earlier."

"Is this about the Rothko?" I asked, too many coincidences lining up for my liking.

"Sort of. Can I meet you this evening? I don't want to discuss this on the phone. I need your help."

"Not tonight." Kolya—quite reasonably—wouldn't be impressed if I abandoned our romantic evening to nip out for a cosy chat with de Bruin. "How about tomorrow morning? I'll go running. You know the houseboats at Little Venice?"

"Yes."

"I'll see you around there on the towpath about ten. That okay?"

"Fine." And he hung up. I put my phone back in my pocket, shaking my head, wondering what on earth he wanted to talk about.

I walked on, slowly by London standards, just enjoying the afternoon sunshine and looking forward to seeing Kolya later. It had been weeks since we'd seen each other, and I hoped that the next few days would reassure me that there was nothing to fear about letting our relationship become more serious.

I sensed my follower before I saw him, some sixth sense sending a shiver down my spine. Spinning round, I scanned the surrounding walkers, searching for a familiar face. And then I saw him; the man from the hallway at Sokolov's house. The one who hustled the girl with the bruised face out of sight. He looked to be in his late twenties, heavily built in a lifting weights and taking steroids way, dressed in jeans and trainers. Surprisingly, he didn't seem to mind that I'd seen him, didn't look away or fiddle with his phone, just carried on strolling towards me with his hands in the pockets of his hoodie.

Walking on, a little faster now, I decided to ignore him. We weren't that far from Sokolov's house; it wasn't completely unfeasible that he should have decided to take a break this afternoon and get some fresh air in the park. It was a coincidence, I told myself.

Pausing at the park exit, turning to cross the road, I allowed myself a glance back and saw him still some twenty yards behind me. I crossed, weaving between gaps in traffic, hoping that I'd shake him off.

I reminded myself that there was probably nothing sinister about his behaviour. Sure, I had an ex who was persisting with some low-level stalking despite a restraining order, but that was no reason to fear any man who happened to be taking the same route as me. Maybe it was just chance that he'd seen me and was following out of curiosity, or maybe he was just enjoying seeing that he'd unsettled me. I forced myself to slow down, take my time, and not let him see my discomfort.

Turning another corner, I crossed the road so that I had an excuse to glance back along the street. He was still there. My pace quickened a little, my instincts over-ruling my brain, a prickle of cold sweat between my shoulder blades.

And then I heard the welcome rumble of a taxi and stuck out a hand as I saw its yellow light hove into view. I jumped in, told the driver to go and glanced at my shadow as we passed. He still looked unperturbed at having been spotted and the cold malevolence in his eyes made me shiver.

7

Belgravia was as leafy and peaceful as ever. Getting out of the taxi, I paid the driver and looked around at the high railings guarding the garden square, the immaculate white-painted stuccoed houses, and the uniform of the nanny escorting the expensively dressed children across the road. The hotel that Kolya liked to stay at was a trio of converted townhouses—small, luxurious and close to everywhere we wanted or needed to go. As I walked through the front door, opened by a liveried footman and breathed in the lily-scented air of the foyer, the tension I'd felt after spotting Sokolov's hired muscle following me ebbed away.

"Miss Carpenter, welcome back to The Chippenham," the manager said as he approached.

"Thank you. It's lovely to be here, as always, Mr Harrison." And it was. Every time I'd stayed here the service was amazing, the food perfect, and our suite the most comfortable place imaginable.

Mr Harrison escorted me upstairs to the Regent Suite with its views over the gardens, the trees turning to gold as autumn drew on, a little behind Edinburgh's seasons. The sitting room opened onto a plant-filled balcony, there was a dining table that could seat six, should we decide to entertain, and even a baby grand piano.

On the vast upholstered footstool between two sofas was a tray with a pile of art books and a vase of yellow roses. The bookshelves were stacked with recent titles and there was a beautiful bureau in case either of us felt the need to write letters on our personalised stationery. The bedroom was vast, the marble bathroom was luxurious and stocked with expensive unguents. If heaven could be a hotel room, then this was it.

Next time I was travelling for work and all I could find was a grotty motel, I'd remember this suite and weep a little. Kolya liked to claim that he could rough it when necessary and that he remembered the privations of the Soviet era from his childhood, but it was a very long time since he'd stayed anywhere other than a five-star hotel.

I asked Mr Harrison to have someone bring up coffee and started to unpack. Kolya's belongings were already in place, his leather washbag in the bathroom next to one of the basins, a book on a bedside table. We had space in each other's homes—the ceremonial allocation of drawer space when you know a relationship will be more than a fling—but there was an intimacy here in this equally shared space. I liked it and wondered whether it was something I should consider on a permanent basis, as Kolya regularly suggested.

A vase of my favourite white roses had been placed on the dressing table, the bedroom full of their delicious scent. Inside the envelope propped against it was a card:

"My darling Kate, I'll be back at six. I adore you. x"

. . .

Once I'd unpacked, my mind wandered back to the stolen Rothko, or rather the stolen not-a-Rothko. That disappointed me. I'd never hunted a Rothko and would have loved to have one on my trophy shelf, especially as the idiosyncrasies of this theft would have been a challenge I'd have relished.

Assuming I was correct in my assessment, I wondered how Sokolov would take the news that I had spotted the forgery. Not well, I suspected. In fact, did he already suspect that I might have spotted the con he was trying to pull and that was why one of his minders had been following me?

After a while, I grew tired of considering the unpleasant Mr Sokolov's motives and took a long bath with lots of The Chippenham's oils and potions and then took a nap. At about five-thirty, I realised that although I wasn't the type to be lounging around in seductive lingerie when Kolya returned, I probably should make a little more effort than greeting the lover I hadn't seen for a month in leggings and a washed-out Radiohead t-shirt. So I put on some underwear more suitable for company and a baggy cashmere jersey. Casual, but he'd be in no doubt as to what my plans for the evening were.

At six o'clock precisely, while I lay on the sofa reading, I heard someone enter the suite and looked up from my book. As always, no matter how much I tried to play it cool, my heart leapt at the sight of him. With a body still as perfect as it was back in his classical ballet prime, and smiling at me from the doorway in faded jeans and a blue linen shirt that brought out the piercing cornflower of his eyes, Kolya was utterly irresistible.

"My darling, I'm not late, am I? I've been so looking

forward to seeing you." And then I was in his arms and nothing else mattered in the world.

We didn't sleep much that night between making love and catching up on the trivia that sometimes got forgotten given the patchy nature of our time together. When you were always aware of the clock ticking down to the next flight that would separate you, it was too easy to stick to the edited highlights, but it was the insignificant details that gave depth, forged a bond, and created a relationship.

Over champagne and smoked salmon sandwiches in bed, Kolya laughed as I told him about my sister's threat to visit me in my very grown-up, very white, flat with her Ribena-spilling toddlers and he told me that his daughter had been offered places at both Harvard and Stanford universities. We talked about plans for Christmas in a few months—Kolya suggesting that I might like to spend it with him in New York—and then he asked what I'd been up to earlier that day.

"A painting was stolen and Joe asked me to look at the crime scene. Nothing exciting, but it was a Rothko and you know how I wouldn't be able to resist that," I said. Kolya had accompanied me on a couple of my pilgrimages to see paintings that were new to me and understood my emotional connection to the works. "But I think it was a fake, so nothing more to do there."

"Who did it belong to?"

"Yuri Sokolov. If I'm right, I don't envy Joe having to tell him the bad news." I laughed but a frown crossed Kolya's face.

"I'm glad you're not working for Sokolov. He has a nasty reputation."

"It's not quite that simple, darling. Joe has me on a retainer and puts a lot of work my way so I don't like to pass on too many. Besides, if I only worked for people of impeccable morals, I'd have very few clients."

"Your clients put you in danger." I could hear the tone in his voice that usually led to an assertion that I should give up my art recovery work and spend more time with him. And there was some truth in his argument, I had to concede. Reminding him that if I had to take any risks, I had a team of decidedly over-protective former soldiers to look after me wouldn't reassure him either. He never asked, but I knew that he was curious about my relationship with Pete and, quite rightly, suspected that it had been rather more than the "brief fling" that I brushed it off as.

"Not often. And I like my job," I said firmly, hoping he'd drop the subject. "And what of your day? What was this mysterious meeting you came all this way for?" His trip had surprised me. He was busy at the moment and generally if people wanted to interview him or discuss anything, they went to him. Getting on a plane for a single meeting was unusual.

"Not now. It's complicated and I need to explain it to you properly. I'll tell you over lunch tomorrow." He moved, stretching a leg and wincing a little.

"Everything okay?" I asked, placing my glass on the bedside table.

"Just my knee. I have to have surgery on it in a few weeks."

"Again?" I ran my fingertips over his leg, tracing the scars of previous surgeries.

"It's either that or give up dancing altogether. My movement is affected and I'm already past my best. Audiences will think I'm an old crock." I knew a review that described him as the "once-great Ivanovich" had stung him.

"You're still incredible. You know that. Don't be self-pitying."

"You're biased, my darling." He shrugged and smiled, knowing it was true. "Besides, with respect, you know nothing about dance." He had a good point there. My only experience of dancing amounted to a handful of lessons when I was about five, my fairy princess dreams almost immediately replaced by a passion for ponies.

"I know genius when I see it." I spoke matter-of-factly. "I know artistry. I know that I can't take my eyes off you even when you're just warming up. And I know that sometimes when I watch you dance, I'm moved to tears." Kolya looked surprised; I'd never told him this. Then he smiled, soft and intimate and irresistible.

"And when I move like this?" He kissed me, pulling me closer, his thigh sliding between mine. "How does this make you feel?"

8

I left for my run early the next morning, having made a vague excuse to a still-sleepy Kolya and promising that I'd be back in time to change for lunch. He'd booked a table somewhere I knew was expensive and said that he had exciting news. I hoped that it wouldn't involve putting more pressure on me. Hopefully, I'd also see his news as exciting and we could have a lovely afternoon together before heading to the Eardisley Gallery party that evening.

The roads were busy with tourists and shoppers and running was hard work, requiring constant changes of direction and pace. I was glad to reach the towpath where there were only other runners and a few rather assertive swans to deal with.

My phone had been buzzing while I was running and I slowed down to a walk so I could check my messages. Most of the calls had been from Joe and eventually he'd left a short voicemail—he wouldn't know the final results of his expert's tests on the strip of canvas until the next day but so far it looked as though I was correct in my judgement of it as a forgery.

Joe sounded pleased about that, no doubt thinking of the millions of pounds his company didn't need to pay out. I didn't envy him telling Sokolov, though. From what I knew of him, he wasn't the type of man to take it well. Joe also informed me that Sokolov wanted to meet with me to discuss my plans for tracing the Rothko. I was hopeful the expert would confirm my suspicions and thus I wouldn't have to have any more to do with Yuri Sokolov. Never mind his history; there was something in those cold eyes that unsettled me.

As I walked, I looked out for Lucien de Bruin. We'd met a few times but I wouldn't consider him a friend. More an acquaintance to pass the time of day with at an auction or private view.

And his reputation was decidedly shady, hence suggesting this as a meeting place, away from people and CCTV. He wasn't someone I wanted to be seen having cosy conversations with just after a multi-million-pound painting had gone missing. On the other hand, he wasn't someone I would expect to call and ask for help. To say that I was curious was an understatement.

I recalled a tall, dark-haired, well-dressed, athletic man with a smile that could break hearts. Spotting him ahead of me today, he looked less suave, almost scruffy, in a fleece and jeans with walking boots. When I drew near, I saw that he was unshaven and his eyes were ringed with tiredness.

"Hey." I stopped beside him and he started, not having

recognised me as I approached. He looked too exhausted even to be vigilant.

"Hi." He paused, seemingly at a loss for what to say now that I was actually there. "Um, thanks for meeting me."

"That's okay. I was in town anyway. What's the problem?" I was brisk, wary of what he might try to draw me into.

"I'm in a difficult situation." He was nervous, eyes flicking around the trees as though checking I'd come alone.

"I assume this is about the stolen Rothko?" I took care to sound matter-of-fact, not giving anything away. "You said you saw me at Sokolov's place. Were you watching to see who turned up?"

"Yes. But I didn't take the painting."

"I didn't say you did. But you know, there's CCTV and the method of entry is your style. Not many people go for the show-boating of going across the rooftops." Now, looking at him, I didn't think he was the figure on the CCTV —he was taller and broader in the shoulder. But I wasn't going to tell him that.

"True. But I didn't do this. Besides, I injured my ankle a couple of months ago. I'm not up to running around on rooftops at the moment." He sounded annoyed, as though he expected me to take his word for it. A bit rich.

"You have a solid alibi? You were caught by another camera somewhere? You were safely and demonstrably at home in Amsterdam?" I was getting impatient, not at all sure why he wanted to meet me.

"No. I was in the UK but out in the country. No cameras, no way to prove it."

"Alone?"

"No. But she has a partner. It's complicated. I don't want to cause trouble for her."

"You might have to cause trouble." He looked even more downcast, and I realised that he'd been banking on me believing him.

When I'd first heard about the theft, I'd wondered if he might be the culprit but I'd dismissed that because I couldn't see his motivation. Lucien was that rare thing, an honourable thief. Relatively speaking. If the stories were true, then he confined his light-fingered activities to short-cuts regarding the recovery of looted and stolen art. He was also good at it. He would know that taking that Rothko canvas and getting away across the roof would be risking his neck and I couldn't see him doing that.

I sat down on a bench and he joined me, leaning forward with his head in his hands.

"Why are you so worked up over this?" I asked. His attitude seemed rather overly dramatic to me. "This isn't the first theft you've been linked to. If it wasn't you, there won't be any physical evidence. And this married woman you were with can give you an alibi if you need it. The police won't take it any further." I shrugged.

"I don't think Sokolov will be as easily put off as the police." He looked at me, worried. "Someone's got hold of my number and his—what's the word? Enforcers?—are threatening me unless I return the painting. If you really believe that it wasn't me then I need you to tell him so."

"You think he'll believe me?"

"Maybe. Obviously, if I had taken it, there would be no clues. I'm better than that."

"Obviously," I echoed. You had to have a grudging admiration for a thief who took such pride in his work. I was willing to concede that it wasn't him on the CCTV, but as for the rest, I couldn't be sure he wasn't involved in some way. I wondered what evidence had been recovered from the scene. As well as the police, Joe's investigators who included former SOCOs, had been over the place. If de Bruin had been there, they might have managed to pick up a trace of his DNA.

"You'll have to leave this with me." I wasn't making any undertakings, and I still wasn't completely convinced of his innocence. "Give me your number. You withheld it when you rang me." I gave him my water bottle to hold as he dictated and I tapped it into my phone.

"Thanks."

"Don't thank me. I'm not making any promises but if I'm sure you had nothing to do with it, then I'll make that clear to Sokolov and Joe. I'll be in touch."

I left him sitting on the bench, a man out of ideas, and started to jog back the way I'd come, holding the bottle by the neck and wondering what on earth I was getting myself into. I felt sorry for Lucien, if his story was true. I'd seen Sokolov's "enforcers" and they weren't people I wanted calling and threatening me. He should have just left town though; a few anonymous weeks lazing on a Bali beach while all the fuss died down would have been a sensible choice.

Once around a bend in the towpath and out of sight, I stopped and pulled a small plastic bag from my pocket. I usually had one somewhere; one of my 'you never know' habits, rather like the toolkit in my handbag. I dropped the bottle in the bag and tied the top shut.

Even if the police had found prints at Sokolov's place, they wouldn't share their findings with me or Joe, and the opportunity to get Lucien's prints on file was too good to pass up. Besides, the police probably didn't have anything of his to compare their findings to. He was too good for that. But when he was off-guard and vulnerable, he wasn't good enough to avoid giving me a set of prints, maybe even a DNA profile.

True, it was taking advantage of a man when he was down, but I wasn't about to just accept his version of things. I was good at my job. But I didn't get good by being nice.

9

We arrived a little late at the restaurant for lunch, but despite its waiting list and reputation, the maître d' had held our table—people always waited for Kolya, I'd noticed. It irked me that he sometimes assumed that I would be just as tolerant.

Although we took our seats with the least possible fuss, Kolya turned heads as usual. It wasn't just the dance enthusiasts, people who'd never heard of him noticed when he walked into a room. A vainer woman might have resented being almost invisible beside him; I just accepted it, preferred it even, and teased him about it afterwards.

"So what shall we do today?" I asked when the waiter had brought us champagne and menus. "A walk in the park? The National Gallery?" I was looking forward to some uninterrupted time together.

"You don't need to work? The stolen painting?"

"Nope. Not today."

"Good. We can do whatever you like. A gallery, then back to the hotel for a nap before we go to the party? And then a late dinner?" I smiled at the way he raised his eyebrows when he said "nap".

"Sounds perfect." We raised our glasses to toast each other, and for a brief moment, I felt completely and utterly content. The waiter took our order and Kolya looked at me, expectant, ready to reveal his surprise.

"Tell me, have you thought any more about my suggestion that you move to New York and live with me?"

I choked on my champagne. This was normally a subject that we circled warily for a day or so, not a grenade to lob into the conversation before we'd even had lunch.

"Well, um. Not really."

"I have something to tell you that might make it an easier decision." Kolya smiled broadly.

"Go on then." I was wary. Although I was happy, Kolya was becoming annoyingly insistent that our relationship should become less long-haul.

"I've been offered the chance to move the company here, to London. An arts organisation wants to build an international reputation for contemporary dance, and they have asked if I would consider basing myself in the UK. I met them yesterday. It's a fantastic offer—lots of sponsors and funding, excellent rehearsal and performance spaces, full artistic control. They'll even arrange all the visas and accommodation for the company."

"The dancers will want to move?"

"Of course." He shrugged, not having contemplated that the dancers, stage managers, dressers, his assistants, and all the other people who kept the company functioning wouldn't be willing to move continents.

They would, naturally. Kolya was a perfectionist, both in terms of his own work and what he expected of his dancers. He worked them until their feet bled, but the result would be incredible. It was what had made him a legend and why those dancers would give anything to join his company. Sometimes I sat in the stalls during rehearsals, and watching him work was captivating and inspiring, even a little intimidating in his intensity.

"Crikey. That would be quite a feat of organisation," I said, playing for time.

"I said that I would have to talk to you before I made a decision. So there you are. The future of modern dance in this country is in your hands." He laughed, without arrogance, but he wasn't entirely joking. "We can live together, be a proper couple." Then, less emphatically, but still rather rashly in my opinion, "We could even get married."

I recoiled at that. Marriage wasn't something I was even close to considering, and we'd never talked about it before. When my mother had found out that we were seeing each other from some photos of us holding hands in the street that made it to a tiny article in the Side-bar of Shame ("legendary dancer Ivanovich out and about in New York with much younger partner"), she'd sent me links to newspaper articles about his rocky marriage to another dancer and their vicious and very public divorce. To cut a long story short, she'd ditched Kolya for a toy-boy and taken his Manet with her.

Given my cynicism about relationships, I didn't think either of us were anybody's bargain on the marriage front.

"Do you have to decide immediately?"

"No, they'll wait." Of course they would.

"Then let's give it some time. Please?"

"Time for what? You must know how you feel by now. It's been over six months. I want to be open about our relationship and committed to each other. I want to be able to refer to you as my partner, not just my lover. This is like an audition that never ends." His voice grew louder and I noticed the couple at the next table trying desperately to hide that they were listening to every word. Kolya had a tendency to the over-dramatic that met its opposite and equal reaction in my very British horror of causing a scene in public.

"Do you often refer to me as your lover?" I asked, curious.

"Occasionally." He waved a hand dismissively. "I don't have a word for what we are." He lowered his voice again. "I'm almost fifty, I'm too old to have a girlfriend. Or would you prefer that I called you my mistress?" He had a point. It was, as the saying went, time to fish or cut bait. "Is it because of our age difference?" The thought struck him and I smiled as I shook my head, knowing that it was something that played on his mind from time to time, especially as I'd just celebrated my thirty-fourth birthday.

"Not at all. I rarely notice it. You know that. I don't think of you as being any particular age. We just are who we are."

"That's okay then." He looked a little mollified. "So even if we can't decide where to live, can we accept that this is a proper relationship, not just some part-time affair? We can talk about living together again in a few weeks. I can hold off on decisions."

"That's fine." I slid my hand across the table to take his. "I'm not going anywhere. I just get jumpy if things are going too fast."

"And can I refer to you as my partner now?"

"I think you'd better." I smiled. "The alternatives are either tacky or faintly ridiculous."

Our starters arrived and we were quiet for a few minutes, commenting only how delicious our scallops (me) and duck terrine (him) were.

I liked the idea of him living in London, only a few hundred miles away. I knew people who commuted to London from Scotland on a weekly basis. We'd be able to spend a lot of time together, enjoying the domesticity that was so lovely when we stayed at each other's apartments. Cohabiting though, that was a whole different ball game. I wasn't sure if I was ready for us to share a bathroom cabinet and utility bills.

But it was true what I'd said—I had no desire to end things and the people who knew about our involvement seemed to think we were good together. Perhaps it was time to settle down. After all, the main reason I'd ended things with Pete was because our lives were so incompatible in terms of a future together. This, a proper relationship, was what I'd said I wanted.

"Of course, if you move to London, you'll find it easier to work from here. You can concentrate on your consultancy work and stop chasing stolen paintings around the world." Kolya sounded perfectly reasonable, but I looked up sharply, having thought that subject had already been put to bed.

"I enjoy my job. And I'm good at it." Even I could hear the warning note in my voice, but either Kolya didn't, or he ignored it.

"But it's dangerous and unpredictable. Surely, you'd rather be at home more, with me? Not so many risks."

"I don't take risks." An image of the dead man in the park only a few days earlier pushed itself into my mind and I shoved it back out of sight. "Not really. If it looks dangerous, I take back-up."

"You mean Pete. That's another thing. I'd rather you didn't spend so much time with him."

"What?" I laid down my fork, feeling my irritation rise.

"Firstly, I don't 'spend time with him' as you call it. We make arrangements on the phone or by email, meet up, get the job done, and head our separate ways. Last time I saw him I don't think we even had time to chat over a coffee. And secondly–" I took a deep breath. "Secondly, it's none of your business who I work with. I don't complain that you spend your days surrounded by beautiful dancers wearing not a lot in the way of clothing, do I?"

There was a moment's silence, both of us digesting what I'd said. I wasn't willing to put up with his jealousy, nor was I going to go into detail about my feelings for Pete, which were more complicated than I wanted to admit. But I would never be unfaithful to Kolya and that was what mattered. I'd made my decision regarding Pete, for good or ill, even if at times it was only steely willpower that kept me from revisiting it.

"I'm sorry. I just worry about you and I don't like to think of you taking risks." Kolya took my hand as we strolled through the park, takeaway coffees in hand. Lunch had been a little tense and, aware of our eavesdropping neighbours, I'd wanted to get out of there as soon as we could. "And I trust you. I really do. I don't trust Pete, but I don't know him. In his place, I'd be trying to win you back."

"There's no need to worry." I squeezed his hand. "Pete and I get on fine, and believe me, if any part of a job gets dangerous, I couldn't have someone better looking after me."

"Does it get dangerous?" Again, there was the man on the bench worming his way into my mind when I really needed an amusing anecdote to put Kolya's mind at rest. I sighed.

"Not really. It's not as though I'm abseiling down buildings to rescue Monets from evil super-villains. Mostly, I hang around underground car parks. Once we had to wait in an abandoned factory in Belarus for a couple of days. We only had a bucket for a bathroom and it was freezing."

"So why do it?"

"The thrill of the chase, I suppose. Because it's fun and I enjoy the buzz. And I like outsmarting the bad guys. I'd get bored if all I did was look after my clients' collections."

Smiling, Kolya stopped and turned to kiss me, his lips September-cold and tasting of coffee and I leaned in. A movement in my peripheral vision caught my eye and I turned to look.

A man was watching us. Not in the "don't I know him from somewhere" manner that was quite common when people saw Kolya, but in a cold, blatant manner. Not curious, but slightly threatening. In his late twenties, he was heavily built in a lifting weights and taking steroids way, dressed in jeans and trainers. He stood with his hands in the pockets of his hoodie, just watching us.

He was one of Sokolov's minders. A different one to the man who'd been following me the day before. Beside him was the young woman I'd seen in the hallway, bundled up in a quilted coat and skinny jeans. The bruise on her face was still livid, exposed when her hair blew back in the wind.

If he'd been alone, I'd have just ignored him and kept walking, but I felt I'd failed the woman when I'd let her be hustled away the day before. Now, I wanted to speak to her. Letting go of Kolya's hand, I hurried over.

"Are you okay?" I put my hand on her forearm and she flinched. I raised my hands in apology. "I'm sorry. It's just—your face. I wanted to ask if you needed help. The police, or a hospital, something like that."

The woman, in her early twenties, looked at me sadly and shook her head. She glanced at the man with her.

"Don't. I'm all right. I tripped and fell. That's all." Her voice was heavily accented and she spoke as though she were reciting an explanation she'd been told to offer if anyone asked about her injuries.

"Even if it was an accident, you should see a doctor." I ignored the annoyed look on the face of the man with her, and held the flat of my hand up to Kolya, telling him to stay out of this. "Would you like me to take you to the hospital?"

"She's fine. She said so, didn't she?" The man stepped forward, grabbing her arm and turning to leave.

"Really, it's okay." The woman assured me as she looked back over her shoulder at me, hurrying to keep up with her companion. Her eyes gave the lie to her words although I felt powerless to do anything. If she'd accepted my offer of help that was one thing, but I couldn't kidnap her and take her to a hospital if she insisted that there was nothing wrong.

I watched them go, hurrying down the broad path before cutting across some grass to where a black BMW pulled up to the kerb. He bundled her into the back of the car and they were gone.

"Kate, who was that?" Kolya was close by, a hand on my shoulder.

"I don't know," I said. "But I wish I did and I wish I'd helped her."

10

Later, as we got ready to go to the party at the Eardisley Gallery, I slipped out onto the balcony and called Lucien, Wary of my mobile number showing up on his phone in case someone who shouldn't saw I'd rung him, I used the hotel phone. I'd have gone out to use a call box if I thought there were any left in Belgravia. With hindsight, I should have found one somewhere or at least withheld the number I was calling from.

I still hadn't decided whether I believed his claims to have had nothing to do with the theft of the Rothko, and I wanted to keep tabs on him for the moment, just in case I needed to track him down to ask him more questions. The bottle he'd helpfully left his fingerprints on was in the hotel room safe and I was planning to drop it off with Joe the following day.

"Where are you?" I asked when Lucien answered, no preamble.

"I'm on my way back to Amsterdam. I thought that might be best."

"Okay." He'd be easy enough to find there. "Have you heard any more?"

"No. Maybe they've decided to leave me alone." He sounded more optimistic than confident and I remembered the man I'd seen in the park earlier.

"Perhaps. Speak soon."

I hung up and stood for a moment, looking out into the darkness of the garden square, wondering if either of the men who'd been following me was out there. Just as I was keeping an eye on Lucien, did Sokolov have something to hide about the Rothko and was watching me in case I rumbled him? And did he realise that Lucien and I were in contact?

When we'd met the day before, I'd been careful to avoid cameras and people, and I was sure I wasn't followed there. I ran at a reasonable pace and doubted the muscle-bound character in the park could keep up with me. So had he been watching Lucien, recognised me from my visit to Sokolov's house, and decided to switch his attentions to me? Whatever the answer, I hoped that Joe's expert would confirm my suspicions soon so I could wash my hands of the whole business of the fake Rothko.

Turning my thoughts away from Sokolov and towards the prospect of a fun evening with Kolya, I turned and went back inside. Adjusting his cufflinks, immaculate in a beautifully cut, almost-black suit, Kolya glanced up at me and I caught my breath. Running from a relationship with a man who could set my pulse racing with just a look would be crazy, I knew that.

"Do I look okay?" He'd seen my face; he knew the answer to that.

"You'll do." I made a point of never pandering to his ego. At least not when he expected it. Nor was I going to fish for compliments by asking for his opinion. I was wearing a fitted dark red silk top and a vintage black YSL smoking jacket over a short black fringed skirt from Stella McCartney and I felt pretty good. My heels were high and we stood eye to eye.

"I like these outings as a couple." He picked a stray hair from my shoulder. "It will be nice to be open about the fact that we're in a relationship."

"Hmm. But you were a client of mine. I worry that people at a party like this might see it as unprofessional behaviour." I didn't want to get that sort of reputation.

"I'm sure people would understand that you couldn't resist my charm." Kolya smiled and kissed me.

"I seem to recall that I resisted your charm for several months. Champagne on your terrace on a spring evening and the scent of cherry blossom was what finally did it."

"It's a very nice terrace," he said, laughing. "Anyway, people probably realised we were dating months ago. We have chemistry that's hard to hide, I suspect, and we haven't been as discreet as you like to think."

"Probably. Just don't mention the Rothko this evening. As far as almost everyone there is concerned, I just tell rich people what to hang on their walls."

Some events in the trade, private views in small galleries especially, are relatively casual. This evening's event at the Eardisley Gallery was a very different kettle of fish. For starters, it was a party, not an opening, so the guests weren't picked solely for their ability or willingness to drop a hundred grand on a piece of art just because they felt like it. Rather, this was a PR offensive.

Guests included trade types like me, journalists, and some of the wealthier and more glamorous art aficionados, but there was a liberal smattering of celebrities of some type or another. They were there to ensure press coverage for the gallery, as the huddle of paparazzi outside demonstrated.

I supposed Kolya fell into a category of his own. He could afford to buy the art on the walls and he was famous in some circles but at the same time, he hadn't been invited and I had. He was just my plus one, my arm candy, as I teased him in the cab. He laughed, but looked slightly baffled, never having been just that for anyone before.

When we arrived, the party was already in full swing. The men there were in a mixture of good suits, a few in dinner jackets, jeans for a few artists and billionaires, and there were a couple of household-name actors who looked to have come straight from a yoga class. Amongst the women, it was wall-to-wall designer gear—some stylish, some simply for the photographers' benefit, and not a lot of overlap between the two. I was very understated in comparison, but I wasn't there for column inches, my name was on the guest list because of the wealth of my clients and the influence I had over where they spent it.

You could spot the reality starlets by how much flesh they had on show, the Instagram 'influencers' because they never looked up from their phones, and the patrons of the arts because they completely stopped talking when they clocked Kolya. Most of the guests couldn't have put a name to him, and people in the art trade were notoriously insular, but to the more cultured crowd he was a rock star.

The gallery space was pristine, the walls hung with some impressive works that I made a mental note to go back and look at properly another day, but this evening was all about the people, the glamour, and the gossip.

We circulated, sipping champagne and making small talk. Kolya didn't move from my side, his hand stroking and clasping mine. It was nice, but a part of me still felt uncomfortable with this public display of togetherness.

"So good to see you two here," a silky smooth voice murmured in my ear and I left Kolya talking to an actor I vaguely recognised from a TV drama, while I turned to hug Helen.

"I know. Like a real couple." I raised my eyebrows as I kissed her cheek, inhaling Guerlain, and admired her dress —one shoulder, perfectly draped silk jersey. Never mind the fashion victims, Helen was the most stylish woman there. I remembered our student days and how we'd haunted the charity shops of Chelsea for bargain cashmere once she stopped being a Goth. "Not that it was exactly a secret."

"You're a lucky girl. When I first spotted him, ages back, I thought how beautiful he was."

"I suppose he is." I glanced across at Kolya, waving an elegant hand as he spoke, and smiled. "But enough of that. How's business? Have you sold those Matisse cut-outs yet?"

"Not yet. You've still time to snap them up. But can't we carry on talking about Kolya?" Helen's eyes twinkled.

"No," I said firmly. "He'll get big-headed if he overhears you."

"You're no fun. I'll see you at the Carlyle sale."

She kissed my cheek and was gone, her attention claimed by someone else and I turned back towards Kolya, aware that I should rescue him from an orange woman with lots of blonde hair and improbably dark eyebrows who was asking him what he did.

"I'm a dancer," I heard him say as I half-turned to smile at someone waving to me from across the room.

"Really? Are you on Strictly?" The woman flicked her hair extensions and pouted as Kolya squeezed my hand.

"No. I'm a ballet dancer."

"Oh." And she turned away. Obviously he wasn't the right kind of celebrity for her. Kolya moved closer.

"Don't leave me. These women terrify me."

"The ones you need to worry about are over there." I nodded, smiling, in the direction of a group of middle-aged, expensively maintained Chelsea ladies who couldn't take their eyes off him. "Royal Ballet patrons, I reckon. Season tickets for Glyndebourne and I bet they never go to New York without catching something at the Met. All the cultural boxes ticked. They really want to talk to you."

The women, emboldened by my smile, approached. Kolya, always impeccably polite, assumed his most suave manner and I reckoned I could safely leave him for fifteen minutes before another reality show D-lister cornered him, so I slipped away into the crowd.

Across the room, just in front of a striking pair of Bridget Riley gouaches, Joe Cathcart was chatting with a few other men in suits, invited because they were the money men who kept the art world turning. I wandered over, ready to be charming—these were useful people to be on good terms with.

"Good evening, gentlemen. How are you?" They all turned, pleased to see me in varying degrees. The couple who knew who I was, who appreciated that I'd saved their bacon in the past, beamed, one hurriedly snaffling a glass of champagne from a passing waiter on seeing that my hands were empty. The other three hadn't needed my services. Yet. They just looked me up and down, assessing and calculating, wondering what my place was in this world.

"I'm sorry to interrupt, but Joe, darling, could I have a word?" I put my hand on his arm and beckoned him with a small nod. Joe turned to me, shaking his head and smiling, and we moved a little away from the group.

"What can I do for you? It doesn't do my image any harm to have you come over to chat to me, but I can't imagine you want to spend the evening with me and my banker friends when you're here with Kolya."

"Maybe not. I was just wondering whether your expert has confirmed that the Rothko's a forgery?"

"He promised me a written report by the time I get to work tomorrow morning. But yes, he agrees with you. Not necessarily on the background thing, that's not his area, but the paint is wrong. Something about egg white?"

"Rothko sometimes used that as a layer of glaze. But I'm glad I was right. So you're shot of Sokolov then?"

"Yeah, well." Joe looked shifty.

"What?" My tone was sharp.

"I haven't told him about the painting being a fake, but I think he suspects something. He's very insistent that you take on the job of tracking it down. As far as he's concerned, he bought an original, it had all the bits of paper proving it and so on, and it's gone walkabout. It needs finding."

"If he did actually buy an original. I suspect that painting went up in flames when the original owner's house burned down. But I'm sure someone will be willing to take his money while they find that out."

"He wants you to find it."

"I'm too busy, Joe." I shrugged. "I've got a lot on at the moment and I'm not taking on an impossible job like that."

"Sokolov wants to discuss it with you. You can tell him no then, but it would keep him happy if you'd just meet with him."

"And keeping him happy makes him easier for you to deal with?"

"Exactly." Joe beamed at me and I remembered just how much Joe paid me to track down his client's missing artworks. And how much I liked him.

"Okay. A quick meeting, but I don't think it's worth my time. And he's not the most pleasant character." I recalled Kolya's opinions about Sokolov, his henchmen following me in the park, the woman with the bruised face. No, I'd be polite for Joe's sake but Yuri Sokolov was not going to join my client list. "Any more news on the theft?"

"No. The police have gone very quiet and my chaps haven't got any leads."

"Well, it's probably not much use now, but I have a gift to drop off at your office tomorrow."

"What's that then?"

"Lucien de Bruin's fingerprints. Possibly some touch DNA too. Handy to have on file, don't you think?"

"You star. How the fuck did you manage that?"

"Because people underestimate me and think I'm nice." Joe knew never to underestimate me. "Like your friends over there. You tell them I'm an art advisor and that Kolya is my rich Russian boyfriend and they'll dismiss me as an irrelevance. Tell them what I actually do—although I'd rather you didn't—and it would be a completely different story."

"I'm sure it would. Speaking of rich Russians." He was alert. "Over there, look."

He nodded toward some new arrivals and I glanced over. Yuri Sokolov was here. Still wearing dad jeans, but this time with a dress shirt and unfortunate ginger suede shoes.

Beside him was a slim—thin to the point of fragility, really—woman who I recognised from my research as his partner, Olga. If she hadn't looked so sad she'd have been beautiful. Her black dress was short, severe and expensive, like her shoes and tiny clutch bag. They didn't look like a happy couple, and I wondered whether she felt that her costly clothes were worth her almost palpable sadness.

Two other men stood to the side and slightly behind the couple. Obviously hired muscle, their hair was too short, their suits too cheap, and their demeanour too unsmiling for them to be guests. One had been my shadow after I left Sokolov's house and went back to the hotel. The other, the one who'd hustled away the woman with the bruised face, was staring at me and there was a venom in his shark-like eyes that made me shiver.

"He doesn't look friendly. And I don't think he's just leering at your legs, Kate."

"No." I moved round so that Joe was standing between me and my watcher. I could keep an eye on him over Joe's shoulder given that I topped him by several inches in these shoes. "I saw him earlier while Kolya and I were walking in Hyde Park."

"Watching you?"

"Yes."

"That's creepy."

"Isn't it just?" I took a mouthful of champagne.

"I'll speak to you tomorrow. Take care." Joe looked unsettled, and I wondered how much he knew about Sokolov's background. I knew few details but the rumours of violence, corruption, and enemies who'd disappeared were enough to make me wary.

11

Across the gallery, Kolya was still being feted by the ballet fans. There were plenty of famous artists there, not to mention the various celebrities who'd turned out, but in their eyes he was a bigger prize. It was time to rescue him and take my prize home. I slipped into the group and took his hand. He squeezed mine, relieved.

"Ladies, it's been lovely but my partner and I have dinner plans and we're going to be late," he explained, appearing truly regretful. I smiled apologetically and we headed towards the exit, saying just a few brief farewells.

We walked close by Sokolov, standing with his back to the wall, looking bored as he chatted with an art dealer I recognised as someone who talked a good game but didn't measure up to his own opinion of himself. Sokolov glanced across, looking me up and down in a way that wasn't lecherous, but rather darker. He made no acknowledgement that we'd ever met, not even a nod.

With his unfashionable clothes and lack of social skills,

Yuri Sokolov didn't fit into this laughing, glittering crowd. He was only welcome because of his money.

My reading over the last few days had built a picture of a man who knew that ruthlessness, brutality even, not intellect or talent, had got him what he wanted. It seemed to be important to him that he could display his wealth, whether by virtue of his yachts, his artworks, or the price of his girlfriend's shoes.

Olga stood a couple of feet from him, a minder at her elbow. She wasn't talking to anyone and still looked unhappy. I felt a pang of sorrow for her and wished that I could tell her to run, to take nothing and run. There was something about Sokolov and his bodyguards that chilled me.

She looked up sharply as we passed and I felt Kolya pause momentarily, just a fraction of a second, as though to speak to her but he kept walking.

We set off down King's Road, hand in hand. The paps had photographed us, but half-heartedly, just being polite. They'd even had to ask our names, so I guessed we were safe from the following day's Sidebar of Shame. If we didn't escape it, at least my mother would be pleased that I was wearing a skirt instead of jeans. She'd point out that it was too short, but still.

"Did you know her?" I asked.

"Know who?"

"The woman you almost stopped to speak to as we left." I didn't want to mention Sokolov but I was interested how Kolya knew Olga. I spoke lightly, knowing that I risked sounding jealous. Which was frankly ridiculous. If I did that every time an attractive woman smiled at Kolya I'd spend my life in a green haze.

"I thought I recognised her. But I don't think I do. You

know how it is. You glimpse someone and they look familiar, but then you look properly and realise you've never seen them before. Why?"

"No reason. Her partner is Yuri Sokolov. The man whose Rothko was stolen."

I left it at that, not wanting to discuss that damn painting again, or the sad blonde woman, or her supposedly tricky Russian boyfriend. I was happy to concentrate on enjoying what was left of the evening with my own tricky Russian.

We stopped for dinner and after more champagne and Dover sole, we got a taxi back to The Chippenham. It had been a lovely evening and having abandoned any public pretence that Kolya was merely a client that I was on friendly terms with, it had been more relaxing than many.

As I'd circulated at the party, my eyes were always drawn back to Kolya, seeing him almost as a stranger at times with that little bit of distance, feeling the familiar pull of lust and the thrill, admittedly slightly smug because I am only human, of knowing that he would be leaving with me.

When we'd initially met, the attraction I'd felt was purely physical. The first things I'd noticed about him when we met at that private view were the breadth of his shoulders, the beauty of his hands as he gestured in the direction of a painting, and the way he walked towards me, oblivious to other guests who wanted his attention, when our eyes connected.

I saw him perform soon after, and as I'd accepted his dinner invitation for later on, he'd suggested I come backstage after the performance. Alone with him in his dressing room, the combination of charisma, sweat, and endorphins was intoxicating.

As time had gone on and I'd got to know his complex, sometimes mercurial, sometimes dogmatic personality; his passion for his art that had driven him to leave his homeland while still a teenager and make a new life on the other side of the world; his conflicting combination of humility and outrageous egotism; his humour; his strengths and his weaknesses, I'd fallen for him in a deeper way. Maybe, I'd thought, this was the grown-up, proper relationship I was sure I wanted.

Now, back in our suite, I dropped my jacket on a chair and turned to him as he switched off the lights, leaving the room dimly lit by just a lamp on the piano. We kissed, and he lowered his head to my neck, running the tip of his tongue along my collarbone and up to my ear.

He whispered something in Russian—I don't know what but it was undoubtedly filthy—and my hands reached for the buttons of his shirt as he reached for the zip of my skirt.

The knock at the door was slightly hesitant, but impossible to ignore. Kolya muttered something, impatient and frustrated, and I went to answer the door, wondering what justified bothering us at midnight. Mr Harrison was standing outside looking awkward and distinctly relieved that I was still fully dressed. I suspected he'd seen us kissing in the lobby as we waited for the lift.

"Mr Harrison. How can I help?"

"I'm so sorry to disturb you, Miss Carpenter, but I'm afraid we've had a phone call from the police and I thought it best to come up myself. Apparently, one of your friends has been in some sort of accident and is in hospital. I suggested that it was rather late to disturb you, but the officer was quite insistent. I gather he's been rather badly hurt."

"Who is it?" My heart beat faster, my mouth was dry.

"I'm afraid they didn't say."

"I'd better go." I didn't know whose side I was dashing to, but if I'd been summoned by the cops, I knew it must be serious. "Can you call me a cab, please? Do you know which hospital?"

"Chelsea and Westminster. He will be in the very best hands."

"I'm sure he will." I went back into our room and fished my phone from my pocket. It had been switched to silent and there had been half a dozen calls from a withheld number in the last hour or so. Kolya had heard most of the conversation and was putting his jacket back on. I racked my brains, wondering who it could be. Then I remembered—the only person who knew that I was staying here was Joe. Fear clutched at my stomach and I didn't speak, just shrugged on my jacket and we left immediately.

The roads were quiet and the journey short. I was out of the cab almost before it had stopped, leaving Kolya to pay as I strode in through the automatic doors as fast as my stilettos would let me. I wished I'd taken a minute to put my trainers on.

The A&E reception at this time of night was crowded with drunks and their similarly intoxicated friends, worried parents trying to comfort screaming children, the lost and the forlorn. I gave my name, said that the police had summoned me and we were whisked through double doors into a world of speedy efficiency, drawn curtains, and purpose.

"This way." I followed a nurse between the trolleys and people to a cubicle with two policemen standing outside. One nodded to me, but neither spoke. Presumably, I was to be allowed to speak to Joe first.

"He'll be fine but he's not in a good way, so don't get him agitated." A bleep sounded and the nurse ran off leaving me to push open the washed-out pink curtain and venture in, dreading what might have happened to Joe.

But it wasn't Joe.

Lying on the trolley, hooked up to monitors and drips, with a swollen face, strapping on his ribs, a bust lip, and the thousand-yard stare of shock and morphine was Lucien de Bruin.

12

"You. What on earth happened?" I took a step towards him and felt Kolya's steadying hand on my shoulder, obviously not feeling my tone was suitably sympathetic, given the state Lucien was in.

"I–." Lucien shrugged, but he had no words. It was obvious that he'd been attacked by people who'd meant to hurt him. This was no mugging. And I already had my suspicions as to who was behind it.

"You said you were on your way to Amsterdam, keeping out of the way."

"Yes, well. I lied."

"Evidently." I felt anger rising, overtaking sympathy. Lucien's light-fingered tendencies were well known and I'd risked my reputation by even talking to him about this theft. I could justify it on the basis that I didn't think he'd taken the Rothko, but I still didn't want it to become known that de Bruin and I were given to meeting up for cosy riverside chats. And now that he'd been beaten up, calling me to attend his bedside was presumptuous in the extreme.

Lucien winced, a monitor started bleeping, and Kolya

and I were whisked out as staff in blue scrubs rushed in. Outside in the central area, I sighed, weary and frustrated.

"Darling, who is that man? Why did the hospital call you?" Kolya's curiosity was understandable and as I looked at him, I saw a flash of something else cross his face. I guessed he was wondering whether Lucien was another part of my life that I'd been keeping from him. I saw a couple of cops heading in our direction.

"Not now. Not right now." I gave him a look that quelled his questions and smiled at the policemen. "Officers, can you tell me what happened?"

"Kate Carpenter?" One took out a tiny tablet and started tapping. "We were rather hoping you could shed some light on this for us."

"I don't know what happened. I don't even know why I was summoned here." Giving nothing away was the best thing, at least for the moment.

"There were only three numbers in Mr de Bruin's mobile phone. Yours was the only one with a name by it. And when we checked with the hotel that he took a call from this evening, we were able to confirm you were a guest."

"I see." I could have kicked myself for using the hotel phone to call him. That had been sloppy. "So, has he told you anything?"

"Mr de Bruin says that he was mugged. Although, he has his wallet and phone so they weren't very thorough muggers. Though obviously thorough in other ways."

"So it seems."

"He was found in a car park behind a solicitor's office in Chelsea by one of the staff who was working late. If he'd been there until morning, he might not have made it. Apart from the cuts and bruises you can see, he has severe abdominal bruising and a punctured lung." The shorter one looked up from his tablet. "How do you know Mr de Bruin? Why did you phone him earlier?" His tone made me wary.

"I'm an art consultant. He's involved in the art business. I'm trying to track down a painting for a client and I called to see if he could help."

"It seems odd that if you're just a casual business contact, yours would be one of only three numbers stored in his phone. Do you know if he has another phone?"

"I have no idea and I can't explain how he stores numbers, Officer." I could hear a defensive note in my voice.

"Where were you this evening, Miss Carpenter?" The tall one this time.

"I was at a party at the Eardisley Gallery, then my partner and I had dinner and went back to our hotel." I looked at them both sharply. "There are plenty of witnesses —hundreds of them—and as you can see, I'm hardly dressed for mugging people."

"I wasn't implying that, madam." He bridled visibly. "But Mr de Bruin's explanation isn't convincing. We hoped you might have some idea as to what happened."

"I'm sorry. I've only met him a few times. Maybe in the morning he'll be able to tell you more. I can't imagine he'll be going far any time soon. And I wouldn't have thought that whoever did this will be back to finish the job. It sounds as though they could have done that earlier."

"Quite." The short one looked up from his note-taking again. "The thing is, I don't think it was a mugging. Do you know why someone would want to harm him?"

"I have absolutely no idea, Officer." I looked him straight in the eye and lied through my teeth. I knew who'd done this, although I wasn't sure why. If you thought he'd stolen your painting and you wanted it back, half-killing him wasn't going to help matters. At least, not until after he'd returned it.

The police officers left soon after, not before taking mine and Kolya's details and giving clear indication that they thought I was holding something back.

The Ivanovich charm worked its usual magic, and a nurse, all giggles and hair-flicking, brought us mugs of tea—hot, strong, and sweet. Despite this smiling conversation with the nurses, Kolya was quiet towards me and I knew I'd have yet more explaining to do later. I groaned inwardly.

The whole hospital thing was making me uncomfortable. It was my first trip to A&E since Chris assaulted me almost two years earlier. Three punches to my face, a kick in the ribs when I fell to the ground and more besides, had left me with an assortment of injuries including a cracked cheekbone.

I'd pretty much put it behind me, but here, with the scent of the antibacterial hand rub, the familiar swish of curtains on metal rails, the wails of the pained, it was all coming back. Nausea made my head swim a little and cold sweat prickled my shoulder blades. I was glad of the tea.

After a while, Lucien's curtains were swept open again and we were told we could go back in to see him. He didn't look much better than before everyone rushed in.

"How do you feel?" I asked, leaning against the wall, arms folded. He nodded without much conviction.

"Not great. But I'll be okay. Just bruises."

"You have a punctured lung, Lucien. That's more than just a bruise."

"Well, yes. I suppose so."

"I wish you'd gone back to Amsterdam and kept out of the way, like you said you would."

"I couldn't. I'm sorry the police called you. I didn't tell them to, but I was pretty out of it." He was distracted, his attention caught by something over my shoulder and I turned around.

Standing about twenty feet away, looking more fragile than ever in the stark fluorescent lights, was Olga, Sokolov's unhappy girlfriend. I looked from her to Lucien and things started to click into place. I took a step towards her and she ran. Swearing under my breath I took off after her, stopping after a stride or two to kick off my shoes.

Outside A&E, I looked up and down the long corridor but Olga was nowhere in sight. Seeing a sign for the exit, I thought that was my best option. I sprinted as fast as I could, and as I came round the corner I saw her ahead of me by the exit. No longer in the severe black dress and Louboutins, she was wearing trainers, leggings and a hoodie and looked quite different. If Lucien hadn't given the game away I might not have spotted her. I ran towards her but Olga had a good head start and by the time I reached the doors, she was in a cab and speeding off.

I walked back to A&E, joining up the dots and coming up with more questions than answers. Rather than thinking that he stole his Rothko, maybe Sokolov suspected Lucien was planning to steal his girlfriend and he'd been beaten up to warn him off. Or maybe Sokolov wasn't aware of the affair between Olga and Lucien and genuinely thought he was behind the theft. But how would he even know of Lucien and his reputation?

Kolya was waiting outside Lucien's cubicle, holding my shoes and he didn't look happy. Lucien could wait until the next day, I decided, now I needed to go home and fill in the gaps for Kolya. I put my head around the curtain.

"I'll be in to see you tomorrow, Lucien. And you'll need to be honest with me about a few things."

"I can't tell you anything."

"You probably should. Goodnight."

I left and went back to Kolya. He gave me a tight half-smile.

"Are you okay?"

"No," I said. "I'm really not. I feel as though I'm being dragged into something against my will."

"Would it help to talk to me?" He put an arm round my shoulders and I leaned into him.

"Maybe, maybe not. But I'll tell you all about it when we get back to the hotel."

"Okay." He handed me my stilettos. "Come on then, Cinders. Let's go." And he took my hand and we walked out to find a cab, me carrying my shoes, too weary even to put them on.

13

Next morning, despite not having gone to bed until after three following a long discussion with Kolya about what had brought us to Lucien's bedside, I woke before dawn and was out running by seven, trying to chase away my sluggishness with exercise and sharp autumn air. As I ran, I kept an eye out for Sokolov's hired muscle but there was no sign of him. Not an early riser then.

Today's plan was to tie up some loose ends regarding the Rothko and then get back to enjoying my time off with Kolya. Somewhat predictably, he wasn't happy about the first part of that. But I'd assured him that after this morning I was done with this. What was the Polish proverb? Not my circus, not my monkeys. Sokolov's fake Rothko was definitely not my circus. Nor, to be honest, was Lucien's involvement with Olga, but I wanted to warn him to be careful there, just in case the collapsed lung hadn't already made that clear.

. . .

When I returned to the hotel, my usual six miles later, a still-sleepy Kolya was drinking coffee and reading the papers. His hair was rumpled, slightly damp.

"How was your run, darling? Coffee?" He took off his glasses and reached out for the cafetière on the tray beside him.

"No thanks, I'll take a shower first."

"You want company?" There was a twinkle in his eye. Perhaps today he was feeling more relaxed and accepting of my activities?

"Maybe, but haven't you just had a shower? Your hair's still wet."

"Can't take too many showers. Cleanliness is important." He grinned, putting the paper down.

My phone bleeped. Joe:

"You still coming into the office this morning? My expert has news and our chum Yuri's been nagging me to set up a meeting with you."

I sighed and replied:

"He's fresh out of luck then. If the painting's a fake, there's nothing I can do. I'll be in with your gift from Lucien but I'm done with Sokolov."

"Joe? Or Lucien?" Kolya's voice was sharp, the seductive tone of a moment ago gone.

"Joe. Just checking I was still calling in at his office."

"And will this take all day?"

"Hopefully not. I have people to catch up with. I should be back here early afternoon."

"Are you sure? Because you said that you would have plenty of time for us this week and yet it feels as though much of it is being taken up with this stolen painting."

I didn't like his tone. This felt like a road I'd been down

with previous boyfriends who felt I should account for my time. And it wasn't a path I was willing to retrace my steps along.

"I'm pretty certain. I'll let you know if I'll be later than that." There was a warning note in my voice and I hoped he heard it. I sat down on the footstool in front of him. "Joe puts a lot of work my way. He has me on a retainer and he—or rather, his clients—pay me a small fortune to find their missing artworks. Sometimes that means I have to prioritise that over time off with you. At the moment, there are some loose ends with the Rothko business that I need to tie up." I shrugged.

"Can't he get someone else to help?"

"Probably. But he'd have to use people who aren't as good as me." I grinned. "Look, I know you're worried after what happened to Lucien but like I said, that was probably about Olga, not this theft and I'm perfectly safe. Sokolov's just pushing his luck, wanting to be the alpha male." I leaned forward, hands on his knees. "If we're going to make this relationship work, you need to accept my job, and that sometimes I'll be talking to people or going places you don't like. In the same way that I accept that your schedule will impinge on our lives."

"But I don't do anything dangerous."

"True. But that's rare. And you know I'm careful. If a situation looks dodgy, I always take minders."

"Pete, you mean." Ah, so this was going to be another issue, I realised.

"Not this again. I'm not willing to stop working with him because you don't like it. He keeps me safe and you have to learn to trust me."

"Of course, I trust you." Kolya looked annoyed. "But I don't like you taking risks. And I don't like you changing our plans when we're supposed to be spending time together."

"Sorry, I'll try not to, but that's how it is. I'm not willing to be in another controlling relationship. If you can't accept that, then maybe we need to think seriously about the future." And I left the room to shower and get changed, wondering if this relationship was also doomed to go down in flames.

Arriving at Joe's premises, I ignored the sleek front-of-house area and headed for his more chaotic office at the rear. My plan was to confirm that the Rothko was a fake, decline Sokolov's invitation to meet and discuss the painting, distract Joe with the plastic bottle, and do a runner. I armed myself with a coffee from the machine and went through to Joe's office.

"Ah, Kate. You're here."

"I am. Your expert agrees with me then?" I sat down opposite him and waited expectantly.

"He does indeed. You made your judgement based on the way it was painted but he's looked at the science." Joe handed me a sheaf of papers and I started to flick through the findings—layers and composition of paint and glazes, preparation of the canvas, manufacturers and dates of pigments, and so on. "I've emailed Sokolov with the bad news." He pulled a face.

"It's not drawn the line you hoped it would?"

"No. Glossing over the fact that he wants to know how we got this bloody sample to test, he's now convinced that someone swapped the paintings and that his original Mark Rothko has been stolen as well as the forgery."

"Really?" I couldn't hide my smile. "Did you explain that

no-one's going to break in, take the original and substitute it with a near-identical copy, and then return to lift the fake one?"

"I have." Joe smiled, charming with a slight wariness in his eyes. "But he's convinced and says he wants someone to track down the original. You, that is. He wants you to find it."

"No."

"He says he'll pay twice your usual fee."

"He can offer five times my fee but I'm still not doing it." I leaned back in my chair, unsmiling. I was lucky enough to be picky who I worked for and Sokolov wasn't going to make the cut.

"I know. But he won't take my word for it. He would like to talk to you and asked—surprisingly politely, I should add—if you would kindly spare him an hour of your time. He says that he thinks the two of you may have got off to an unfortunate start and he regrets that."

"Bollocks he does." I nearly choked on my coffee. "What do you think?"

"I agree with you. But he's expressed a willingness to settle this business once and for all and drop his claim once he's discussed it with you. And I would love to open my emails without expecting to see another slightly threatening message from him." Joe shrugged. "Give me time, I'll ditch him as a client altogether."

I could see why Joe wanted me to take the meeting. Stifling a yawn, I considered it.

"Tired? You need some early nights." Joe grinned.

"I tried to last night. Trust me. Life had other plans, though." I explained about Lucien's admittance to hospital and Olga's unexpected appearance in the casualty department.

"You reckon she's shagging de Bruin?"

"You have such a delicate turn of phrase, Joe. But yes, I suspect she probably is. And the girlfriend of a man whose painting might have been stolen by her bit on the side? That's interesting, don't you think?"

"Too right. And this meeting?"

"Okay. Kolya and I are going out for dinner this evening. I can give Sokolov an hour at six-thirty. You need to come, too. Then, I'll get a cab to my date and I don't want to hear another word from him or about him." I could imagine what Kolya's reaction would be, but if it drew a line under all this, it would be worth it.

"Thanks, Kate." Joe looked grateful. "I'll check times and be in touch."

"That's the time I'm free. Six-thirty. It's a one-time-only offer." Not wanting to discuss it further, I delved in my bag and produced the water bottle, still in its plastic bag. "This should cheer you up. Lucien held it for about thirty seconds. You should get fingerprints and a palm print. Your lab might even get some touch DNA. Handy to have on file for the future, perhaps?"

Leaving Joe pleased with the bottle, I left, not wanting to devote any more time to discussing Sokolov. Most of my clients were delighted that I was able to help them. They paid my not-insubstantial fees and expenses without quibbling and even if I didn't manage to negotiate for the artwork's return, they were willing to accept that I had given it my best shot.

Sokolov's attitude that I should jump when he snapped his fingers did not encourage me to take the job. He was not a man accustomed to being told "no" but he would have to get used to it when it came to that painting.

. . .

Understandably, having schlepped across central London from Joe's office, I wasn't best pleased to discover that Lucien had discharged himself from hospital earlier that morning, less than twelve hours after arriving in an ambulance.

"Really? But he had a punctured lung." I couldn't hide my shock and the nurse shook her head.

"I know. We advised him to stay here but he wouldn't listen. Mr de Bruin is reasonably stable and should be okay if he rests, but I told him I couldn't be sure. We can't keep people against their will, more's the pity." She rolled her eyes. "The police arrived to talk to him again, just after he'd left."

"Did he give you an address where he'd be staying?" I asked, a little knot of worry forming in the back of my mind.

"Are you a relative?" A flicker of suspicion crossed the nurse's face as she realised that she may have already said too much and I paused. What was I? Certainly not a friend.

"I'm a colleague."

At that point, she became more professional and distant, presumably as she remembered why the police wanted to talk to Lucien and realised that I might not be as kindly as I first appeared. She wasn't going to tell me where he'd gone. I hoped he was on his way to Amsterdam and that he'd make it; he'd looked dreadful the night before.

I strode the couple of miles to the Chippenham in a foul mood, stopping off to buy a cheap pay-as-you-go mobile in case I needed to call Lucien again. Paying cash, naturally. I'd gone to the hospital full of questions for

Lucien about how, exactly, he'd ended up beaten and unconscious.

It didn't take a genius to work out that it was something to do with Olga and why she'd run when she saw that I had questions. But how could she have known he was there? Had Sokolov or whichever of his men was responsible let it slip?

When Lucien asked for my help to exonerate him for the theft of the Rothko, it seemed there was a lot he hadn't told me. And if I was getting hauled out late at night to his bedside and followed by Sokolov's hired muscle, then he was going to damn well give me some answers.

14

Bracing myself for another sharp exchange with Kolya, even less in the mood for his possessiveness or sulking than I had been that morning, I arrived at the hotel and picked up my messages from the front desk. There was one from Kolya because he couldn't get me on my phone to say that he'd be back late afternoon. And one from Joe arranging to pick me up at six.

Up in our suite, I showered off the London grime and curled up with a book. I thought about calling Lucien, just to see where he was and that he was safe, but decided that his problems could wait. And once I'd told Sokolov where to get off this evening, Lucien would no longer be of interest. He could look out for himself. He wasn't a friend and I owed him nothing.

Nonetheless, I couldn't help wincing at the sheer viciousness of the attack on Lucien, remembering the woman I'd seen in Sokolov's hallway and the park. What was her role in the set-up? She wasn't glossy and expensive like Olga and she didn't look comfortable with the man who'd hustled her away from me, so probably not his girlfriend. She'd looked scared and the injuries to her face indicated she had reason to be.

When I'd been that woman with the bruises, I'd had help from friends, police, and lawyers. I wished I'd done something for the woman at Sokolov's house. I considered ringing the police, but the realist in me knew that they couldn't do anything. People were wary of men with Sokolov's power, and my concerns were mostly based on impressions rather than facts. I didn't even know her name. Despite the stab of guilt, all I could do was park my worries and hope that I ran into her a third time. If I did, then maybe I could persuade her to let me help her.

Kolya arrived a little after three. I put my book down and looked up from the sofa, assessing his mood, wondering whether to be ready for another row. I didn't like this feeling of wariness.

"You're back, darling. I'm sorry I wasn't here." He bent to kiss me, energetic and full of life. Unlike the elegant tailoring of the previous evening, he wore jogging bottoms, trainers, t-shirt and hoodie, a small rucksack over his shoulder.

"That's okay. Where have you been?" My tension ebbed away immediately. He might be a little demanding but I knew he would never leave me with broken bones like Chris had.

"The London Ballet Theatre. I felt restless and I know the director so I called him to ask if I could borrow a studio. They didn't have anywhere free, so they moved a rehearsal to the main stage in order to give me some space. So kind. I've been stretching and doing barre work, practising a little. I had to strap my knee but I've worked out some knots and I feel much better. I get grumpy when I haven't practised for a day or two."

"I've noticed that." My tone was dry. "I'm glad you feel better."

"I do." He sat down next to me. "And I'm sorry about earlier. I shouldn't have been possessive. I worry about you, but I have to respect your choices."

"Good." I got the feeling he'd been rehearsing that on the way back to the hotel.

"We're partners and I have to accept that you can't devote all your time to me." He said this as if it were a major revelation. I shook my head, amused. "What's so funny?" His tone was a little sharper.

"You are. You're almost fifty and you've just realised the world doesn't revolve around you." I pulled him close and kissed him. "You've spent too much of your life surrounded by people who will move heaven and earth for you."

"That's not true."

"You don't even notice. Look at today. Would any ballet company say no to you if you wandered in and asked to borrow some practice space? Of course not. They would recognise you immediately and do anything to avoid disappointing you."

"If you say so." He seemed unconvinced.

"More to the point, have you ever dated a woman who wouldn't drop everything if you called?"

"I don't know. Probably." He didn't sound sure and I doubted it very much.

"Hmm. I'm not so sure, but if we're going to make it past Christmas, you have to understand that I won't always be available. It's been fine while it's mostly been long weekends like this—" I waved a hand at the hotel room, "but if you want us to be a proper couple, then you have to accept the fact that I will sometimes be busy with other stuff. And I may not be able to tell you much about it for confidentiality reasons. Just as I know there are things in your life that are important to you, that you can't change."

"I don't like to think of you taking risks."

"So don't think about it." I grinned and he kissed me again. His skin was salty with sweat from practice, a sharp tang on my tongue. Then he pulled away sharply.

"Do people really do that? Rearrange things to suit me?" He was genuinely puzzled.

"Kolya, in your world you are a god. You don't even realise how people smooth your way. Look at your assistants and what they do for you. You don't even make your own restaurant reservations or doctor's appointments. But you're not a god to me, just a man, however much I adore you."

"Darling?" I opened my eyes as I felt Kolya's lips on my shoulder and rolled towards him, smiling. He was holding out my phone. "You have calls."

The screen showed that Joe had called four times in the last hour or so. As I looked at it, his number flashed up again.

"I'm sorry." I smiled apologetically.

"Don't worry about it. I'll leave you to it." He left the room, humming softly, much more relaxed than I would have expected. Maybe he'd been listening to me?

"Hi." I tried to sound awake.

"At last. I thought you'd lost your bloody phone. And that hotel reception is no help whatsoever."

"What do you want Joe?" I flung over onto my back, wishing I could hang up and drift off to my post-coital sleepy place again.

"It's Sokolov. He changed the time of the meeting to six,

so I'll be at your hotel in a cab at five-thirty." Joe sounded apologetic.

"For fuck's sake. He's just playing games, you know that, right?"

"I know. We'll be shedding him as a client ASAP, but for now, let's go along with it."

"Okay. I'll see you later." I hung up and groaned as I glanced at the clock. It was already a quarter to five. I rolled out of bed, pulled on a t-shirt and went to look for Kolya. He was in the sitting room, idly flicking through the newspaper and turned to me with a broad smile.

"Everything okay?"

"Kind of. You won't like this but I don't have time to discuss it. Joe's picking me up shortly because I've agreed to a meeting with Sokolov. Just to tell him that I'm sorry his painting was a forgery but I won't be hunting for the real one."

"You're right, I don't like it."

"Nor do I, but it's politic to go. I'll be an hour or so. Tell me what restaurant we're having dinner at and I'll be there by seven-thirty. And then there will be no more Yuri Sokolov in my life."

"Sure?"

"Completely."

I disappeared to the bathroom, took a quick shower and got dressed—posh underwear, a sleeveless silk vest, skinny black trousers, a leather jacket and Valentino ankle boots. I twisted my still-damp hair up into a loose French pleat and threaded my diamond earrings into my lobes.

Kolya, emerging from the shower as I was putting on lipstick, looked me up and down.

"You look great."

"Thank you. If you recall, we're going out for

dinner once I've dealt with this. Sokolov only warrants jeans and trainers, these are my going on a date with you clothes."

"Good." He kissed me. "I can't persuade you to ditch the meeting and come back to bed?"

"Oh, I wish I could, darling. But I need to do this for Joe. Besides, I spotted the forgery and it will be nice to see Sokolov squirm a little when he realises exactly how much I've cost him."

"That was very sharp of you."

"I told you, I'm good at this."

"A whole new side to you. Very badass, very sexy." He nuzzled my neck.

"Well, you keep thinking that and I won't disillusion you." I didn't want to go into too much detail about the surveillance stints in leaking buildings and the crappy coffee and the roach-ridden hotels, preferring to maintain the impression that it was at least partly down to piercing insights and private jets.

15

"You know, when you said he wanted to meet us at a club, I imagined the Groucho or Soho House," I said to Joe as the taxi drove off leaving us on the pavement in the West End, islands in a tide of hurrying pedestrians, looking at an old repurposed bank. "The St Petersburg", it proclaimed in gold across the doors, and on a plaque to the side in smaller letters "exclusive adult entertainment". It didn't look as though it had much in common with the city I'd visited the week before.

"Shit. I'm sorry, Kate." Joe shook his head. "He's playing games. Let's go."

"It's fine. He wants me on the back foot, embarrassed, so I'll agree to what he wants just to get out of here. But it takes a lot more than this to make me uncomfortable." I nodded to the doorman. "And look at the sign; at least it's 'exclusive'. Clearly, it won't be even slightly seedy." I grinned at Joe and took a couple of steps towards the door. He hung back slightly.

"My missus is going to be furious if she finds out I've been to a lap dancing club."

"Will she mind less if you tell her you were with me?"

"Possibly, although I'll have to do some explaining as to why you were here." Joe shook his head. "You'll need to back me up. She likes you."

"Of course I will. Come on, we'll keep this as brief as possible." I squared my shoulders, smiled at the doorman who rushed to open the gilded door for us, and we went inside.

The club was an odd combination of some rather nice Victorian detailing; stone columns, marble floor tiles and so on, overlaid with black walls and a neon sign behind the bar with the name of the club in the Cyrillic alphabet. There was a thin layer of glitter over everything, and the air was a heady cocktail of thumping dance music and perfume. I suspected its claims to be exclusive were all very relative.

Ranged around a catwalk-style stage in the centre, complete with chrome poles, a dozen or so men—city types mainly—sat at tables, talking and disinterestedly watching the women who were strutting their stuff on stage in various states of undress. It was early; I imagined things got livelier later.

A woman approached us, a hostess rather than part of the entertainment judging by her neatly tailored black suit. She smiled, not incurious about me.

"We're here to see Yuri Sokolov," Joe said, pointedly not looking around in case his eyes fell on naked flesh. "Is he here?"

"Of course. He said that he was expecting guests. He's in the Amber Room, please come this way."

We followed her towards the rear of the club, past a

dancer spinning upside-down around a pole with a core strength I envied, down a short corridor, and were ushered into a gold-painted room with black leather sofas, chrome poles, and a rather poorly executed painting of a naked woman. It was as similar to Peter the Great's famed Amber Room, lost to looting Nazis, as Lambrusco was to Bollinger. Outside, the door was guarded by a couple of heavies, all muscle and buzz cuts.

In the middle of the largest sofa, flanked by a pair of fawning, skimpily dressed women sat Yuri Sokolov. The sweatshirt and dad jeans had been replaced by a shiny suit with an open-necked shirt and well-polished dress shoes, but he still lacked any vestige of style.

"Ah, Miss Carpenter. Welcome to the St Petersburg." He didn't get up and I wasn't about to stand before him like an employee who'd been summoned. I took a seat on the sofa opposite him, fighting the urge to brush off traces of body glitter first, and smiled politely.

"Mr Sokolov."

"What do you think of the place? It belongs to a Russian friend who wants me to invest so he can expand. He plans a chain of these in all the major cities of the world. It's a new investment area for me, adult entertainment, but it's classy, isn't it?" He was smiling and expansive, but there was a sharpness in his gaze, my responses noted closely.

"I'm sure it is, but I'm not familiar with strip clubs so I have nothing to compare it to." I crossed my legs, refusing to look ruffled. Joe stopped hovering at my elbow and sat down beside me. "I gather you wanted to discuss your painting."

"Yes, my Rothko."

"Your fake Rothko." I couldn't resist poking the wasps nest a little.

"That was very clever of you. You cost me a lot of money,

you know?" He took a bottle of champagne from a bucket and poured me a glass, handing it to one of the women who placed it on a side table next to me. He topped up his own glass but didn't offer any to Joe.

"I expect it did. I'm sorry, but I work for Joe's company, not you. And it would be unprofessional of me not to speak up, a disservice to the artist as well, don't you think?" I didn't pick up the glass.

"Perhaps. But the fact is that I bought a Rothko painting and if the one that was stolen was a forgery, then my original is missing."

"It's possible." I shrugged a little. "I think it's more likely that someone sold you a fake in the first place."

"Impossible. I inspected that picture myself. It must have been substituted for the forgery." He was getting riled now, offended that I thought he wouldn't know a fake from the real thing. Catching the eyes of the two women, Sokolov gestured for them to leave with a curt nod of his head.

"I suppose that's possible," I conceded, although in my opinion the chances of that were negligible.

"Either way, I bought a painting, and the original is out there somewhere and I want it found. I'm told you specialise in recovering stolen artworks." Although his posture seemed relaxed, his pebble-grey eyes were fixed on mine.

"I do."

"And I'm told you're very skilled at that."

"I am." I maintained my polite half-smile, waiting for him to get to his request so that I could decline and Joe and I could leave, drawing a line under this whole business.

"I wish to hire you to find my painting." Still those eyes, hard and unblinking. I felt a prickle of goosebumps on my arms, uncomfortably close to his barely contained malevolence.

"I'm sorry but I'm very busy at the moment. The cases I already have need my attention and I can't let my consultancy clients feel neglected. Also, like I said, it's quite possible that the original painting no longer exists, that it went up in flames with the owner's house all those years ago." I was still polite and professional, resisting the urge to be rather blunter and leave fast.

"Mr Cathcart said you might decline. I will double your usual fee. And pay a bonus if you find it." Sokolov's eyes narrowed a little, and I remembered the girl with the bruised face in his hallway, the way he'd sent his minders to follow me, the sadness in Olga's eyes, Lucien's collapsed lung. No, I was never going to work for this man.

"That's very generous but as I said, I'm not able to help." I went to stand up, already aware that this was a conversation destined to go round in circles.

"Name your fee." Sokolov's tone was harder. In his world, everyone and everything had a price. Except me, it seemed.

"Really, no." I got up. "I can recommend a couple of other art recovery specialists who might be able to assist." Joe rose too, saying nothing, letting me handle this.

"You don't think that since you've already cost me so many millions of pounds, you owe it to me to find the real painting?" Sokolov's body language had changed subtly; his posture was the same but there was a tension in his shoulders and an irritated tap of his fingers on the hand that sprawled along the back of the sofa.

"I owe you nothing, Mr Sokolov." I shouldered my bag, and he stood up, taking a step towards me. Every instinct told me to back away, but I stood my ground, maintaining a polite expression. He oozed threat, but I wouldn't let him see my discomfort. "I wish you the best of luck in finding the painting, though. It's beautiful and I hope it did survive the fire."

Sokolov didn't speak, just regarded me coldly. I didn't hold my hand out to shake his as he didn't appear to be feeling cordial. And I didn't want him to touch me.

"Goodbye, Mr Sokolov."

"Well, hopefully, that's an end to it." A yellow-lighted taxi hove into view and I waved. It pulled up and I nodded to Joe to get in, preferring to talk inside rather than in the street outside a strip club.

"I bloody hope so." Joe sounded weary. "I just want to walk away from this, Kate. All those threatening emails and demands on the phone. I've seen you and Pete when you pull off a job, high on adrenaline, but my idea of excitement is a close game of golf on a Saturday morning. I like my quiet life in Surbiton with Ellie and the kids. If I wanted danger, I wouldn't have gone into insurance."

"Of course, if this doesn't shut him up, one way to get rid of him would be to find out who took his Rothko. Then, his focus would move from you to the thief."

"Do you know who took it?" Joe's voice was sharp as if he suspected I was keeping something from him.

"No. I don't think it was de Bruin, though. Although, he's been less than honest with me, so I wouldn't rule him out completely. Anything on those prints of his?"

"Not yet."

"Good to have them on file for future reference. Hopefully, Sokolov will give up now and leave us both in peace."

"Thanks a lot, Kate. I appreciate this."

"It's okay, it's what you pay me for." I leaned forward to ask the cabbie to stop.

"Have a good evening. Sorry if this has spoilt your break with Kolya."

"Doesn't matter. It's good for him to realise that he's not my only priority. And besides, I don't like loose ends."

I arrived at the restaurant before Kolya, took a seat at the bar, and by the time he got there I was sipping champagne. I watched him walk towards me, his gait graceful and measured, his shoulders broad beneath his jacket and smiled. He leaned in to kiss me.

"How was your meeting?"

"Short. Thankfully." I decided to avoid going into details about the venue. "Sokolov asked me to name my price for tracking down the painting and I said that I was too busy. That's it."

"So, I have you all to myself now?" He raised an eyebrow.

"Pretty much. I'd like to go to the auction at Carlyle's tomorrow, but I'm not bidding. I want to get a feel for the market, see what sells and who's buying. But yes, essentially, I'm all yours until you go back to New York."

"Good. I don't want to share you." Kolya smiled and kissed me again, and I bit back the flicker of disquiet his words triggered, reminding myself that he was not Chris, that he would never hit me if he felt that he was not my priority. Then he reached out, brushing something from my thigh.

"What's that?" I asked. He looked puzzled, squinting at his hand.

"It looks like glitter."

16

Carlyle's Impressionists and Modern Art Evening Sale was a smart event. I didn't want to seem as if I was trying too hard, but I needed to make a vestige of effort. In the end, I went with black trousers, my Saint Laurent jacket, and a top that I'd bought in a hurry in Paris and which was rather more transparent than I expected, plus five-inch heels in case I wanted to look down on anyone.

"What do you think?" Forgetting my usual rule of not asking, I struck a pose as I fastened my earrings and Kolya paused, assessing me. Sometimes he really didn't realise which questions were rhetorical. He was wearing dark jeans, a white open-necked linen shirt, and a black jacket, with his hair just rumpled enough, and the reading glasses I found surprisingly sexy poking out of his breast pocket.

"You look great. But you know that I can just about see your bra through that top?"

"I think that's the idea. Are you complaining?" I heard the sharpness in my tone. My mother criticising what I wore was one thing. I didn't expect it from a boyfriend. Or partner. Or lover. Or whatever term we'd decided to go with.

"Never. I like it. It's hot." He pulled me to him and kissed me hard, hands on my waist. "There's something that outfit still needs though." He took a small red leather box from his pocket and my heart started to pound.

"What's that?"

"Don't sound so worried. I went shopping after practice because I wanted to give you a gift to symbolise our changing relationship."

"That's nice." I could feel my chest tightening. Surely he hadn't forgotten what I'd said about taking things one step at a time. How did that warrant jewellery?

"It's okay, I'm not going to propose." Kolya smiled. "When I do that, my darling, I'll go down on my knees and do it properly. But in the meantime, I hope you'll wear this as a token of my love. A statement of intention, if you like." He opened the box and took the ring from it. "You choose which hand."

I couldn't hold out my left; the thought of that and all that went with it terrified me. So I held my slightly shaking right hand out to him. Kolya slid the band of platinum and diamonds onto my third finger and I stared at him, lost for words. Then he kissed me.

"Thank you. It's beautiful." I looked at it again. It was gorgeous; simple and quite plain while also being a socking great diamond ring. Nothing discreet about this.

"In Russia, wedding rings are traditionally worn on the right hand. So you can wear it there if you like, but every time I look at it I'll be seeing an engagement ring." He grinned, pleased with himself. "But I'm not putting any pressure on you."

I raised my eyebrows at that. He wanted me to move in

with him, he was proposing to relocate his entire dance company across the Atlantic to be with me, and he'd just spent heaven knew how much in Cartier. Meanwhile, I hadn't got to the stage where I could say "I love you" and was regularly plagued by worries that I'd made some mistakes along the road that brought us here. Yeah, no pressure at all.

I loved the buzz of an auction house before a big sale. Even if I wasn't looking to bid, it was interesting to be in the room and feel what the temperature of the market was —who was bidding and who wasn't. Were those prices being slowly teased out by the auctioneer or were people clamouring to buy? And the gossip was always rife at sales; you never knew what you might hear.

Everyone was keyed up, excited about the paintings they hoped to buy, nervous in case they weren't the highest bidder, wondering what the works they were selling might fetch, and calculating outcomes on their fingers to see which of the three Ds (death, debt, and divorce) would be settled by the sale. And the staff were hyped-up with a mixture of excitement and stage-fright, the fall of the hammer possibly representing millions of pounds in commission.

Fairs like Art Basel and Frieze were interesting and an important part of my annual routine, but there wasn't the same anticipation and, just like when I hunted stolen paintings, I loved the adrenaline of competition.

As soon as Kolya and I arrived and had drinks, I saw Helen who hurried over to greet us.

"How lovely to see you, darlings. You must sit next to me during the sale, Kolya, so that I can tell you tales of the disgraceful exploits Kate and I got up to in our art school days."

Kolya seemed keen to hear more and I let them chat while I looked around. There were some dealers I knew slightly and other advisors milling about with mobiles glued to their ears while they spoke to their clients in a dozen different languages.

My phone rang and I looked at the screen. Jason:

"Hi, how's tricks?"

"Kate, are you at the sale?" The line from Palo Alto wasn't the clearest.

"At Carlyle's? Yes, we've just arrived. They'll be getting underway in about half an hour."

"There's time, then. I want the Picasso. You gotta buy it for me."

"Jason, it's too late. We talked about this and you agreed to let this one go. We were planning to check out the spring sales in New York." I spoke quietly, smiling so that no-one saw me hissing at my client.

My eyes flicked across the room to where the Picasso in question hung in prime position next to the auctioneer's rostrum. It was a wonderful piece. I reached over to shove my glass into Kolya's hand and snatched the catalogue from Helen. Thumbing through one-handed, I found the details for *Femme en Sommeil.*

"I know that, Kate, but you said this was a good one. It's gonna look great in the guest suite and my mom loves abstract art. I can surprise her."

"I'm sure she'd love this." How could she not?

"Exactly. We should buy this one. My gut tells me so and I always listen to my gut. It's made me rich enough to be able to afford that painting. Can you get it for me?"

"Maybe. I think so. But it's late. They might have

someone free to take a telephone bid. Otherwise, I'll have to bid myself in the room. I don't like doing that on a major piece."

"You'll be fine. Don't be nervous." Jason adopted a soothing tone.

"I'm not nervous." I was sharp with him. "But I prefer to be on the phone because if I'm seen bidding and people remember that you're one of my clients, it could push the price up." I threaded my way across the room, beckoning to one of the auctioneer's assistants. "Hang on, Jason. Stay on the line."

"Miss Carpenter?" The assistant was bright-eyed and smiley.

"My client wishes me to bid on a painting. I wasn't expecting this. Can you organise a paddle for me, please?" She ran off, and I spoke to Jason again. "That's Lot 39. What's your limit?"

"The guide's 25 to 35. What do you think?"

"How many millions do I think you should spend on a painting that neither of us has had a good look at? I don't know Jason, how crazy are you feeling?" I laughed. "How much do you want it?"

"Can you see it?"

"Yes. From across the room, but even at a distance it's breathtaking." I looked down at the catalogue description, scanning the immaculate provenance. "Carlyle's is as trustworthy as they come and there isn't anything in the painting's history that's vague or fudged. It's a good example of his work from that period, very commercial if you want to sell it in the future, and I think you could be quite bold." I was trying to sound professional despite being caught on the hop.

"If you had my money, how much would you spend on it, Kate?"

I walked towards the painting, loving the rich colours, the symbolism, the work of a genius at the peak of his powers. It lit up the room. I fell in love.

"It's amazing. If it were my money, I'd pay whatever it took, Jason."

I'd given up on trying to sound detached and objective. Normally, my clients and I talked about purchases well in advance and agreed a budget that balanced the likelihood of being successful with not paying over the odds. I hated having things sprung on me like this, leaving me with no time to prepare. If I screwed up, my reputation could be badly damaged.

Spending this sort of money without proper discussion and actually inspecting the work fully was crazy. But I knew that this painting would blow Jason away when he saw it in person and it would be an amazing addition to his collection. The assistant came back, clutching a form and a paddle with a number on it.

"I have to go. Text me a limit and I'll do my best." I hung up.

"We have all your identification on file, Miss Carpenter, so you just need to sign this. Here's your paddle. I'm sorry but the sale's very busy and it's so late that I don't have anyone free to be on the phone with you or a box you can use." The young woman looked slightly taken aback by my sudden arrival. At big sales like this, unexpected bidders didn't tend to walk in off the street, especially serious ones intent on buying one of the star lots.

"Not to worry. Thanks."

I took the paddle and the catalogue and made my way back to Kolya who was still holding my glass and talking to

Helen. From their wary expressions, I suspected I looked less than happy.

"Darling, what's wrong?" Kolya put his hand on my arm. "Who was that on the phone?"

"Jason. He wants me to buy a painting for him. He's just decided."

"That's short notice. Which one?" Helen asked.

"*Femme en Sommeil.*" I tried to look relaxed and casual to other observers.

"Lawks." She smiled, amused.

"Exactly. I have to bid for it in plain view, as well. You know I don't like doing it this way. I prefer the phone or to be up there." I nodded upwards at the circle of boxes where the super-rich and super-secretive who liked to bid themselves could do so screened from the *hoi polloi* downstairs.

"You'll be fine," said Kolya, soothing. I glared at him.

"Of course, I will. This is my job. I just don't want other people pushing the price up." I was annoyed but didn't need to be reassured that I could manage. Helen squeezed my hand.

"Come on, let's get our seats. Where do you fancy?"

We picked a spot at one side, about two-thirds of the way from the front. I had a clear view of what was happening and if I wanted to move, I could easily slip out to stand at the back of the room.

I checked the provenance again. I'd pointed out the painting to Jason when the catalogue first came out but he hadn't been sure and I'd suggested waiting until he saw a Picasso that really spoke to him. With a few exceptions—a Leonardo or a Vermeer would be one-time only possibilities—it was always better to wait. It might take a while for the right painting to come up at the right time, but it was preferable to rushing in and regretting a purchase later. My plan to take Jason to the New York sales so he could take some time to properly view the works was a good one. Spending this sort of money on the spur of the moment because he thought it would look nice in his guest bedroom was less than ideal. My phone buzzed as a text from Jason arrived:

"I really want the Picasso so go up to double the top of the guide if you need to. My Mom is gonna love it! x"

17

I showed the text to Helen, who tried to hide a smile. Kolya leaned over from my other side to read it, and smirked.

"So what's your plan, darling?" Helen asked, looking forward to some entertainment.

"Honestly? I don't have one. I suppose I'll see what the initial interest is and go in strong once I start. At least that budget should cover it." I smiled and composed myself. I'd spent more in the past, but doing my bidding via one of the fearsomely efficient auction house staffers on the bank of phones at the side, while I maintained an impassive expression and spoke to them in single syllables from the back of the room was a lot less stressful. I wasn't shy, but I preferred to keep a low profile. Dealers saw me in galleries and sometimes at sales with my clients and would draw their own conclusions, but purchases were very rarely explicitly acknowledged.

Kolya was making polite conversation with a culture-vulture who recognised him and Helen nudged me.

"That's an impressive bit of magpie bait on your right hand."

"Isn't it?" I looked down, the diamonds sparkling in the bright lights.

"Wrong finger for an engagement ring, so...?" Helen lifted an elegantly arched eyebrow.

"Apparently, it's a symbol."

"A symbol of several carats. Taste and generosity and the arse of Michelangelo's David; he really is the perfect man." Helen smiled. I knew that she was right and wished there wasn't a warning bell somewhere in the back of my mind. Instead, I looked down at the catalogue, gripped my bidding paddle and hoped that 602 was my lucky number.

The stage was set. The auctioneer and his staff were conferring, the seats filling up, the screen that would display the current prices in half a dozen currencies was in plain view. Some of the more dramatic pieces hung on the black walls beautifully illuminated by spotlights, and there was a rather lovely antique easel set up to hold other smaller artworks. Nearest the rostrum was the Picasso, the nude's heavy-lidded eyes as she dreamt of her lover shielding her from the vulgar gaze of those who saw her value in solely monetary terms. It was a stunning piece.

Robert Follett, one of my favourite auctioneers, was selling this evening and there was a sudden expectant hush as he took his place on the platform. Good-natured and first-rate at his job, he made people feel relaxed, easing just a few more million from them even on the slowest day.

The initial lots went for decent prices, comfortably above their lower estimates and a fair few clearing the top of the range given. I felt calmer and looked around the room, seeing if I could spot anyone who I thought might bid against me. And I wondered who I couldn't see—they were the real threat.

During the bidding for Lot 15, a Degas pastel of a pair of dancers very similar to one that hung in Kolya's apartment, Helen nudged me and nodded in the direction of the far side of the room. A small group were rearranging themselves to accommodate a couple of late arrivals—Yuri Sokolov and Olga. They took seats near the front. I looked at Helen and we raised our eyebrows at each other.

I wouldn't have expected Sokolov to bid in plain view but for some collectors, all men I've noticed, there's a huge amount of ego involved in buying art. Personally, I'd always thought their need to wave their money around quite so blatantly was a clear sign that they were over-compensating for something. Sokolov looked around the room, and I leaned back slightly, hoping that Kolya's broad shoulders on my right would screen me. They saw me, though. At least, I saw Olga catch sight of Kolya, glancing across as if she knew him.

"Sokolov's girlfriend, Olga." I whispered in his ear. "That's twice now that I've got the impression that you know each other. At the Eardisley Gallery, I saw a flicker of recognition and she's looked over a couple of times. What's with that?"

"Are you jealous?" He took his reading glasses off, turned his head to look at her, then replaced them and went back to browsing the catalogue.

"Should I be?" I raised an eyebrow.

"Of course not. She looks vaguely familiar, I suppose. Didn't you say she was Russian, too? But why does it matter?"

"I just think it might."

"Darling, lots of beautiful women smile at me. It doesn't mean that I know them."

"You arrogant sod." I jabbed him in the ribs, and he shrugged, smiling.

Around Lot 25, I went to the bathroom and as I washed my hands, Olga came in. There was a moment where, in the mirror, I saw her hesitate as though wondering whether to speak to me and our eyes met. I half-smiled, encouragingly, but she turned away and headed for one of the cubicles.

I had so many questions for her; did she know who took the Rothko, or what had happened to the original, and was she aware that it was a forgery? But I reminded myself that the Rothko wasn't my problem any more. Leaving aside the missing painting, I wanted to tell her to leave Sokolov for her own safety. There was a coldness in his eyes that chilled me and I couldn't imagine that he'd be understanding if he found out she was having an affair with Lucien.

Back in the room, the sale was up to Lot 33 by the time I fought my way back through the throng to my seat. Helen handed me my paddle.

"Has Sokolov bought anything?" I asked.

"No. Just sat there in his nasty suit. He looks as though he's in a foul mood."

"I think it's his natural demeanour." My phone buzzed in my pocket. Jason:

"We're all watching online in the office. Good luck. Go get 'em, girl! X"

I always smiled at the way he thought sales were like rodeos. I suppose you could take the billionaire out of Texas but you would never take Texas out of the billionaire. And luckily, this wasn't my first rodeo.

"Now, a very special piece. *Femme en Sommeil* by Pablo Picasso. Inscribed and dated along the lower edge and completed in 1934. Who'll start the bidding at twenty million pounds?"

Robert Follett looked around, and I saw his eyes flicker between Sokolov and me. His staff had obviously told him that we were the most serious buyers in the room for this painting and he was scenting a battle. Neither of us was known for throwing in the towel. I leaned back a little and crossed my legs, making sure to look relaxed and confident. He dropped his suggestion to £18 million, then seventeen, and sixteen, and at fifteen I casually raised my paddle.

"And we're off. Lady's bid over there at 15 million pounds. Now, do we have eighteen?"

I slid my eyes over and saw that Olga was back. She glanced in my direction and then whispered in Sokolov's ear. He raised his paddle, no rush.

The game was on.

Another few bidders came in on the telephone, the staff having urgent conversations with them behind their hands, not wanting anyone to overhear or lip read. Taking care to look nonchalant, I let the others run the price up to £31 million and then as they dropped out, I caught Robert's eye and nodded.

"£33 million back here in the room. Do I have thirty-five?"

Sokolov nodded and I did the same as the auctioneer's eyes turned back to me. Prompt, no hesitation. £37 million, above the top estimate. Sokolov bid thirty-nine and I nodded again. Forty-one. A murmur among the people in the room.

That's when Sokolov turned to look at me. His eyes met mine and I flashed him a smile. He gave me a look that was far less warm and returned his gaze to Robert on the rostrum, upping his bid to £42 million. I smiled. He'd opted for smaller increments before I did. I had the upper hand now, psychologically at least. I increased my bid to forty-three and the room grew quieter, everyone transfixed as they realised that neither of us was going to go down without a scrap.

I was in a dilemma. My client wanted the painting and had authorised me to spend up to £70 million. It wasn't worth that and I didn't want Jason to pay over the odds because another buyer was willing to outbid me in a fit of ego. But Jason wanted it and ultimately my job was to give him what he wanted. If I dropped out before his limit then I would need to find him a truly amazing alternative. And his mother would be disappointed. I nodded to the auctioneer, I'd keep going for now.

"I reckon it's a safe bet at up to fifty." I muttered to Helen behind my hand.

"I think so."

Another few bids later and we were at £47 million and I waited to see if Sokolov would take it to forty-eight. He did and I bid forty-nine. I thought I'd heard a very slightly hesitant note in his voice. Without looking away from Robert, I texted Jason:

"Are you absolutely sure?"

Sokolov increased his bid to fifty but sounded less convincing. A text came back:

"I trust you. Do it. x."

I nodded to Robert. Again, Sokolov turned to look at me.

Again, I smiled at him, maintaining my relaxed posture by sheer force of will. It felt as though the whole room was holding its breath. Kolya squeezed my hand.

"£51 million against you, sir. Do I hear fifty-two?" Sokolov didn't reply. "Are you quite sure, sir? £51 million to the lady on my right."

"Fifty-two million." I was impressed, and slightly taken aback, by just how much threat Sokolov got into those three words. Robert looked back to me and I nodded. This time, Sokolov didn't counter.

"Selling to the lady on my right for fifty-three million pounds–."

The gavel hit the block and the Picasso was mine. Or rather Jason's. It was a wonderful work and if I would wake up to that in his guest suite, I would definitely accept one of his invitations to visit him in Palo Alto.

There was a ripple of applause and I texted Jason while Robert moved on to the next lot. The three of us slipped out and garnered a few more friends for our celebratory dinner. Kolya kissed me.

"You were amazing. Not a flicker of nerves."

"Almost like it's my job." I kissed him harder, my pulse still racing, wishing we could cut and run and go back to the hotel. He could tell what I was thinking.

"So it's true? Money is an aphrodisiac," he murmured in my ear and I shook my head.

"Never. Winning is the aphrodisiac."

I made my excuses, needing to nip away to a back office and sign some paperwork before I disappeared. Carlyle's would undoubtedly be confident that I—or rather, my client—was good for the money, but it wasn't unknown for bidders to try to renege on the obligations that came with the fall of the hammer. I arranged to call in the following day and organise shipping and hurried back down the hallway to rejoin my group, looking forward to our celebratory dinner. The thrill of battle was fading a little now, but I was still smiling to myself.

Rounding a corner, I nearly bumped into someone coming in the opposite direction and dodged to the side to avoid them, an automatic apology on my lips that died away as soon as I saw that it was Yuri Sokolov I'd almost knocked flying.

"Miss Carpenter." He stopped in the centre of the corridor, blocking my way. "That was quite a victory for you."

"What can I say? My client was very keen to buy that painting. His mother is a huge Picasso fan, apparently." I was smiling, used to these slightly awkward but usually good-natured conversations at the end of a sale.

"You seem to keep cropping up in my life at the moment." He wasn't smiling back. "Always frustrating me. You spotted that my painting was a forgery and then yesterday evening you refused to look for the original, even though I was willing to pay several times your usual fee. And now, here you are again. Defying me once more."

"I'm sorry if it seems like that. It's really nothing personal." My expression was still polite, if less friendly, and I went to move past him, wanting to leave this conversation behind. We would no doubt see each other again, given the circles we moved in and keeping things cordial, if only on the surface, would be best. But he turned, backing me against the wall.

"Let me pass." I wasn't smiling any more, instead I felt a tingle of fear.

"You need to learn your place, Miss Carpenter. You need

to learn not to get in my way." His voice was low, his face close enough that I felt spittle on my cheek.

"Move aside. Now." My voice was firm but he didn't give way and I pushed, both hands on his chest. He resisted and I saw a hand come up as though he was about to hit me. Memories of Chris's attack flashed into my mind and I shoved him harder, making some space between us so that I could turn and run.

I barrelled into the cloakroom and leaned over a wash-basin, bile rising. After a couple of minutes it passed and I took some deep breaths, snatched up a paper towel to mop the sweat of fear from my brow, and waited for my hands to steady. A woman came out of a cubicle and through the mirror I saw her look at me curiously.

"Dodgy prawn, I think," I said, still slightly shaky. "I'd avoid the canapes."

She left with a sympathetic pat on my shoulder, and I looked at my pallid reflection. Sokolov's barely contained rage had brought back memories I'd worked hard to bury. I remembered Chris holding me down, squeezing my throat until I passed out, and it was all I could do to force that fear back into its box. The two of them had the same rage in their eyes, the same anger at perceived slights on my part.

At last, my pulse returned to something approaching a normal rate and my nausea passed. Sokolov's air of menace chilled me, but I told myself that now he'd made his point, he'd let it go and we could keep our distance from each other. In the meantime, I needed to plaster on a smile, join Kolya and my friends, and try to forget that moment of sheer terror.

18

The following day was one of those sunny autumn mornings of crisp air and glowing leaves when all felt right with the world. I left a sleeping Kolya and walked the half-mile or so to Carlyle's where I celebrated my—Jason's really—victory over coffee with Robert Follett and a couple of other senior members of staff. Then I signed a sheaf of papers relating to payment and the shipping of the Picasso to Jason in Palo Alto and strolled back to the hotel, feeling pretty chipper about life.

Taking a short cut down the lane behind The Chippenham, I barely had time to register the figure in my peripheral vision before the first blow struck my shoulder, knocking me off balance and sending me reeling. I dropped my bag and my phone skittered across the cobbles of the mews, my cheerful text to Kolya half-typed. I staggered, wondering what had happened and looked round at the person who'd stepped out from the gateway.

It was my shadow from the park, the minder in Sokolov's hallway I'd seen manhandle the girl with the bruised face, the man Joe had spotted watching me at the gallery party.

And I realised straight away that he hadn't simply failed to see me. The collision was deliberate, and he was coming at me again.

The second blow, open-handed to the side of my face, sent me sprawling, first on my knees and then over onto my back, skinning my palms as I put out my hands in a futile attempt to save myself. Dazed, I looked up and saw him raise his booted foot, ready to kick me in the head, and I rolled fast in the other direction.

Up on my feet now, I was ready for him, but he had several inches and about five stone on me. He wouldn't catch me if I could run but trapped by the door of one of the garages that lined the mews, I had nowhere to go and he was built like the proverbial brick outhouse.

He punched, and I dodged away, getting past him into the more open space of the lane, ready to turn and run. Shaking my head as I tried to clear my fuzzy vision a bit, I looked behind me and saw a big black car parked across the mews with a man, undoubtedly another of Sokolov's heavies, leaning against it. No point running that way. The other end of the cobbled backstreet was empty but my attacker was between me and escape.

Wheeling round, he struck out again, ready for me as I dodged sideways, but this time I grabbed his wrist to pull him off-balance, and kicked, catching him on the kneecap. He cried out and staggered, then came back at me, red-faced and roaring with steroid-fuelled rage.

I had no plan beyond fighting until I could see an opportunity to flee, trying to remember everything I'd learnt when Pete he taught me to spar at the gym. My attacker got a punch in, hard, to my abdomen, winding me and then followed it up with another blow to the side of my head.

Gasping for breath, unable to scream for help, my sight

blurred and the metallic taste of blood in my mouth, I didn't think I'd be able to defend myself against this for long. He was bigger, stronger, and knew what he was doing. That I was a woman didn't bother him in the slightest and I had no idea when, or if, he would stop.

I backed away a few yards, buying myself a few seconds to judge the situation, looking in vain for a way out. Spitting out a mouthful of blood as he came at me again, this time I got lucky.

He slowed as he pulled back his hand and I stepped in close and brought my knee up fast and with all the force I could muster, connected with his balls. As he gasped, frozen for a moment, I punched. The side of my fist collided with his nose so hard that I felt something crunch in my hand, and as he fell, I turned and ran for my life.

I didn't remember much of the next hour or so. Apparently, I burst through the front door of the hotel and collapsed in the foyer, gasping for breath and faint with pain. The police arrived, and an ambulance, and someone fetched Kolya from our suite.

By the time I started taking anything in, I was seated on a sofa in the lounge with a blanket round my shoulders. There were so many people in the room. Kolya was next to me, grim-faced as he stroked my shoulder. I looked up and around the room, squinting as I tried to counter the blurriness in my left eye. My hands were shaking and I felt icy-cold.

"Kate, do you know where you are?" A uniformed police officer was kneeling in front of me. I nodded at her. I was at the hotel, its restrained elegance a marked contrast to my bloodied state. When I'd put my hand up to my hair, it had been sticky with blood. Hopefully, I wasn't bleeding on their immaculate upholstery

"And can you tell me what happened?"

I could remember flashes of violence and pain at least, but I couldn't form sentences, barely words even. I tried, then gave up, shaking my head in frustration, and wincing at the shooting pains caused by that simple movement.

"That's okay. You've taken quite a pasting and we need to get you to hospital." A paramedic was kneeling beside the cop. "You can answer questions later."

"No hospital." I managed to say that, quietly. "I'll be fine." The paramedic smiled gently and shook his head.

"No, Kate. You have to come with us. Your jaw needs to be x-rayed, and your wrist. And someone should look at your eye." As he looked at me, assessing the damage, I could see from his face that I was in a worse state than I thought.

"And we need to find whoever did this." The cop again, insistent. "This mugger is still out there and we've got to catch him before he does this again."

"Not a mugger." Speaking hurt and took such concentration.

"Someone you know?" The cop's eyes flicked to Kolya and back to me so fast I don't think she was aware of it, but even with only one fully functioning eye, I noticed. I knew that she saw too much domestic violence to make assumptions. And I knew all too well that charm and sympathy could hide a darker reality.

"Not him." Someone passed me a glass of water and I drank deeply, my trembling hands spilling a good deal of it on the hotel's expensive carpet.

"So if it wasn't a mugger, then who?"

"It was a warning. Or something like that. I don't know." The reality hit me then. This wasn't a mugging or a warning.

This was a punishment. At that realisation, I started shaking harder, fear clawing at me.

"Who would want to do that, Kate?"

"I'm not sure." I didn't want to say anything else until I'd had some time to process this.

"We need to go to the hospital now." The paramedic was firm and I nodded at him, reluctantly compliant. I looked around. Other police officers were talking to hotel staff, taking notes as they did so. I needed to call Joe. To tell him. To warn him.

"Where's my phone? I dropped it. And my bag."

"Don't worry about that right now. It's probably what he wanted." The police officer was soothing.

"It's got everything on it." I looked at Kolya. I didn't care about the bag but I needed my phone. Even in my dazed state, I knew that there was a lot of information on it that I didn't want someone else to have access to. If it was gone then I needed to wipe it remotely.

"We'll find it." I heard the manager's voice. "I'll send some of the staff out to search. And I'll call Mr Ivanovich if it turns up."

The hospital seemed to take hours. Two policemen waited outside my cubicle, Kolya charmed everyone, which ensured supplies of tea and biscuits from besotted nurses, a succession of kind doctors peered at my face, into my eyes, gently wiggled the fingers of my rapidly swelling left hand, and palpated my abdomen to make sure nothing major had been damaged by the vicious punch that landed there. And I gradually started to piece things together.

I was in shock. I knew that, although knowing it didn't enable me to feel warmer or to stop shaking. The adrenaline of the fight or flight instinct—both in my case—was replaced by fear and pain and thoughts of what might have happened. Wheeled between x-rays and scanners, I complied with all the examinations and answered as many questions as I could or was prepared to. There was a lot I needed to consider before I said too much.

Kolya, beyond the professional tea-generating charm, was quiet, and I could tell he was also shocked. I'd gone out that morning to stroll through the autumn sunshine to Carlyle's to organise shipping the Picasso to Jason in California and told him I'd see him later to go out for lunch. At no point had either of us envisioned me getting jumped in the peaceful streets of Belgravia and left with injuries like this.

He held my intact right hand and stood beside my trolley, a strong, comforting body to lean against. I felt his lips brush my hair at intervals but he didn't try to make me talk and for that I was grateful. He put an arm around my shoulders at one point and I cried out. The first blow had caught me there but I'd forgotten, so much other pain screaming louder. A doctor saw my reaction and I was taken away for another x-ray.

By the time the hospital released me, it was late afternoon. The two burly police officers led Kolya and me out and put us in the back of a squad car. I panicked, heart racing.

"Where are we going? I want to go to our hotel." They glanced at each other before one turned to me. He was about fifty, kind and soothing.

"Our Detective Sergeant wants to talk to you about the attack. She suggested you come to the police station."

"No. I'm not talking to anyone about it. Not yet. Please take us to the hotel. Kolya, make them do that." I looked round at him, pleading while tears pricked my eyes, and he shrugged.

"That might be best. Your sergeant can visit us there, maybe? I think Kate needs to rest before she answers questions. And it's not as though she's under arrest, is it?"

Back in our hotel suite, Mr Harrison fussed over me like a mother hen, bringing tea and ice packs and sending one of his minions to buy arnica for my bruises. The hospital had given me some hefty painkillers and I felt a little fuzzy around the edges. The doctors had also warned me that my injuries would feel more sore and look worse before they got better, so I wasn't looking forward to that.

My bag had been found in the mews, thrown into a corner. The kitchen porter who'd discovered it didn't give it to the police and hadn't realised that whoever had chucked my phone in there might have left fingerprints that would identify my attacker.

Someone had put my phone back in my bag and taken my wallet instead. Probably the accomplice I'd seen waiting with the car. The man who'd actually carried out the attack on me would have needed help, and certainly wouldn't have departed at any speed after the force with which my knee had connected with his testicles.

I looked at the phone with its cracked screen and saw that there was nothing unusual in my notifications, nothing that indicated anyone had heard what had happened to me. Joe had called for some reason and I knew I needed to ring and tell him about the attack on me.

Putting my phone to one side, I drank my tea. So much tea that day.

19

Not wanting to talk, I left Kolya and went through to the bathroom to see what sort of state I was in. My heavily strapped hand was sore although nothing was actually broken, only a cracked metacarpal. No real damage, I reminded myself, just a lot of bruising and pulled muscles.

So far, I'd avoided my reflection. One of the nurses who discharged me told me in a kind voice to remember that my injuries appeared much worse than they were, that in a few days I'd feel better and that most of the bruises would be gone in a week or so.

And then I looked in the mirror above the washbasin.

Although not an excessively vain woman, what I saw shocked me. The right side of my face was sore and swollen, my half-closed eye bloodshot and bruised. I tasted blood again and, poking about with my tongue, I encountered a couple of molars that felt a bit loose.

On the positive side, my jaw wasn't broken, nor the orbital bone around my eye, or the cheekbone that had been cracked once before thanks to Chris.

After a bit, I ran out of positive thoughts and tears welled up. I blinked them back furiously—crying was no help now —and began inspecting the damage to the rest of my body. Awkwardly, trying to avoid using my sore left hand, I unbuttoned my jeans and pushed them down one-handed, kicking them into a corner of the bathroom.

In the full-length mirror, I saw my knees were bruised and swollen from where I'd fallen. I pulled up my jersey to look at my abdomen and in the bruises developing there I could see the shape of my attacker's fist, each knuckle picked out in purple.

I turned, twisting my head round, and there was more bruising to my spine, every vertebra livid. Shoulders, arms, knees, ribs... everything hurt.

My lip trembled and this time I couldn't fight back the tears. I looked as though I'd been in a car crash. But this was no accident; it wasn't down to the simple bad luck of being in the wrong place at the wrong time. Someone had attacked me and might have done worse if I hadn't managed to run away. My knees gave way and I sat down on the side of the bath, sobbing and sobbing, unable to stop.

I don't know how long I cried—ten minutes, half an hour, longer maybe. I was aware of Kolya holding me but I was beyond comfort, needing the catharsis of letting the fear and pain pour out of me.

When the storm had passed, Kolya ran me a bath and washed the blood from my hair, picked the grit from the street out of my palms, and placed the softest of kisses on my forehead. He took the arnica and worked it gently into my bruises before tucking me up on the sofa with a blanket around me.

He barely spoke, just comforting me and caring, and he didn't ask any questions. I was pleased about that. I knew who had done this, and why, but talking about it was something I wasn't ready to do.

Sore in my body and my soul, I felt anger stirring within me. When Chris had attacked me, I'd channelled the trauma into a steely determination to see him held to account. And thanks to police officers and lawyers and my evidence he was. At least for the elements of his assault that I was willing to talk about. The rest of it, well, the only people who knew everything were Pete and the therapist Flora had persuaded me to go to when it became clear I wasn't coping well despite my insistence to the contrary.

This time, the police would be unable to do anything, I knew that. Without a doubt, Yuri Sokolov had sent his thug to attack me and that it was nothing to do with his stolen Rothko painting any more. It was down to my refusal to do his bidding and although for the moment I might let him think he'd won, I was already working out how I would hold him to account.

Joe arrived around eight o'clock, barrelling in, pale and worried, stressed in a different way to his usual near-coronary manner. He sat down on the footstool next to where I was curled up under my blanket.

"What on earth happened?"

"Well," I began, but despite the ice packs I'd been holding to my face, talking was still painful. I'd texted Joe hoping to see him the next day when I might be feeling better, up to speaking whole sentences at least, but he'd insisted on coming straight over.

"Someone attacked Kate on her way back to the hotel. In broad daylight. This, this, is what he did to her. Mostly it's bruising and she'll be fine in a week or two. Her hand will take longer. She was lucky." Kolya was leaning against the windowsill, arms folded, face like thunder.

"The hand was me. Not him. I punched him." I raised my swollen and bandaged hand, needing to make clear that I wasn't a passive victim. Kolya glared at me, and I subsided under my blanket.

"What have the police said?" Joe patted my knee and I winced. Those bruises were coming up fast.

"Kate won't speak to them. They'll be here in the morning and I hope she'll see sense by then." Kolya didn't give me a chance to answer and there was an iciness in his voice. He'd been quiet since we got back from the hospital. I'd assumed he wanted to let me process the day's events, that he was shocked too. Now, I realised his quietness hid a simmering fury.

"Who do you think did this, Kate?"

"For fuck's sake, Joe, look at her! And think about what's happened this week. There's only one person who would be angry enough to send his thugs to do this," Kolya erupted. "You need to persuade Kate to talk to the police and you have to keep her out of this sort of thing in the future."

"Kolya, please." I raised a hand half-heartedly and tried to speak but caught my swollen lip with my teeth and grimaced in pain.

"Did he say that Sokolov sent him?"

"No." I spoke slowly and carefully. "He didn't say a word. But it was one of his minders. He was at Sokolov's house and at the Eardisley party." Speaking hurt so much. I reached out for my glass of water and Joe passed it to me.

"Kolya's right, Kate. You need to get the police involved."

"No." I shook my head and winced. "Nothing will stick. You know that. All we've got on him is attempted insurance fraud. I'll be fine in a couple of days." It was too much talking and I closed my eyes, exhausted. The three of us were quiet for a moment.

"I should go and see him. We can talk about this." Joe and I both looked at Kolya with undisguised horror.

"What are you going to say?" Joe asked.

"That he should come clean to you over this painting. That he should turn over to the police whoever did this to Kate. To remind him that this is not how we Russian men conduct ourselves."

Kolya stood up, tall and heroic. Foolhardy, but his loyalty was impressive. He would walk into the lion's den for me but he underestimated Sokolov and I'd learnt never to underestimate an enemy. They might back down at your challenge, but they could do worse than you ever expected. And Sokolov wasn't the backing-down type.

"No," I tried to sit up properly. "You think he'll see reason, but he's a gangster and he's ruthless. He doesn't have the same moral code as other people."

"Are you saying I'm not man enough to defend you?" There was a challenge in Kolya's voice.

"I know you are. But I don't need you to defend me in that way. Charging round there won't help. I have to think of a way to make him keep his distance."

"And you can do that? By yourself? Without the police? In the state you're in?" Kolya sounded scathing, waving his hands in frustration.

"Yes. No. I don't know. When I've had some rest I'll come up with something." I subsided on the sofa again, weary from talking.

"You're so stubborn. This is ridiculous." Kolya left Joe and me in the sitting room, slamming the bedroom door behind him.

"He's got quite a temper, hasn't he?"

"Not like this, usually."

"Can't say I blame him."

"No, nor me." I closed my eyes.

"Are you really okay, Kate?" Joe knew that I was putting on a brave face.

"No. I'm really not. This has scared me."

"That's what Sokolov wants."

"I know. And I don't want to give him that satisfaction. The police won't be able to touch him for this, but surely he'll back off now that he's made his point?"

"Some point. Look at the state of you." Joe waved a hand in the general direction of my face.

"Quite." My temples were pounding. "I'm going to take it easy for a few days and then go back to Scotland. He can think he's won if that makes him happy."

I lay back against my pillows, drained. Joe shook his head a couple of times and then left, hugging me carefully and telling me to be careful.

Kolya came back to the sitting room, calmer and full of apologies for losing his temper. I knew he had a good point. I'd have been out for blood if he'd been attacked. And I could see why he might take personal exception to Sokolov's actions. After all, they were of a similar age and had spent their early years only a few hundred miles apart, but they'd taken very different paths in life. But while Kolya was an artist, Sokolov had made his money through greed. Kolya was revered for his talent while Sokolov was feared for his brutality.

My phone rang and Kolya reached over to pick it up and pass it to me. It was Pete. The photo of him that flashed up was one I'd taken on holiday a year or so earlier, all bare chest, suntan and lazy smile. Awkward. Kolya said nothing but I saw his eyebrow lift and made a mental note to change the picture attached to Pete's number to something more innocuous.

"Hi, Pete." I tried to smile, hoping he was ringing about something trivial and I could end the call quickly.

"What the fuck happened?" My smile faded. Pete had never raised his voice to me before and the anger in his tone was a shock. Kolya also heard him, loud and clear.

"Who told you?"

"Joe, of course. He's worried sick. He thought I could talk some sense into you. You have to make a statement to the police."

"Why? It won't help. The man who did this is probably out of the country already. You know how people like Sokolov work."

"And what if he sends someone to finish the job?" Pete asked and I heard him take a couple of deep breaths, then, "I'll kill the bastard." Cold and decisive and, to be honest, perfectly feasible for Pete.

"No, you won't. You're better than him. Besides, he's bound to back off now." I'd been trying not to think about the possibility of Sokolov sending someone else after me to finish the job. "Anyway, Kolya's here."

"He's a fucking ballet dancer, Kate," Pete erupted again. "With all due respect, I'm not happy leaving your safety up to him." I saw the look on Kolya's face—he'd definitely heard that as well.

Pete and I spent the next ten minutes debating the question of whether I should allow him to despatch one of his friends who worked in close protection to come and keep an eye on me, how badly hurt I actually was, and my perceived idiocy in insisting that I would be absolutely fine at the hotel.

"I'll be back in Scotland in a few days. Hundreds of miles from Sokolov so that's okay."

"Okay." Pete sighed, knowing he wouldn't budge me on this. "Well, if you change you mind about a bodyguard, let me know. Call me if you need anything. Anything at all."

"I will. Promise."

I wasn't sure that I completely believed my assertions that Sokolov would back off now. I suspected that he was vindictive and enjoyed instilling fear. Empathy was not one of his qualities. But surely, surely, Sokolov would think he'd had the final word now?

Kolya continued to try to persuade me to let the police investigate, to come to New York with him. He even argued in favour of Pete's suggestion of having a bodyguard to look after me. Eventually, unable to cope with any more, I burst into tears.

"I just can't bear the thought of you being hurt again. And seeing you like this makes me ashamed that I wasn't there to protect you." Kolya dropped to his knees beside the sofa, taking my uninjured hand in his, he sounded truly bereft. "I care about you such a lot, Kate."

"It will be fine. I won't take any risks, I promise." I smiled a little, squinting at him with my good eye.

"I'm glad to hear it. You know, it would be so much less stressful for me if you just gave up work and married me."

"So you say. But I'd get bored and probably kill you, so maybe on balance..." I shrugged and he kissed me gently on the lips. "I'll be careful, honest. I won't do anything rash."

And he smiled, reassured, not realising that I had my fingers crossed beneath my blanket. I knew he meant well and he cared deeply, but between him and Pete and Joe, I'd had enough of men telling me what I needed to do.

What I wanted was to have some space to decide on my own plan to deal with Yuri Sokolov, because I had a feeling that he enjoyed terrorising people too much for this to be an end to it.

I needed to take action, not just wait, fearful, for the next attack. I might retreat to regroup, but I wouldn't run and hide.

20

Sunday's train to Edinburgh was slow, the buffet trolley ran out of milk for tea and coffee, and the only functioning loo was at the furthest point from my seat. I regretted my refusal of Kolya's suggestion to hire a driver even before we'd pulled out of the station.

It had been forty-eight hours or so since the attack. My left hand in its strapping was proving awkward; I'd always assumed that I was more ambidextrous than I actually was. But although the bruises on my body were fading, my face was another story. The swelling had gone down and my vision was clear once more, although I still looked pretty battered, a fact confirmed by the horrified and curious glances of my fellow passengers.

I was stiff and moving gingerly, but I felt as though I was on the mend. Physically, at least. I hadn't left our suite since we returned from the hospital and when we set off for Kings Cross, I found myself scanning the streets through the taxi window, wary of who might be watching, a knot of fear in my stomach.

"Be careful." Kolya had seen me onto the train and we

said our farewells by the door as the guard walked along the platform. “Call me when you get home.” I could see the worry on his face, the frown lines between his eyebrows. I promised to do so and waved as the train moved out of the station, suddenly feeling very alone.

As I settled in my seat, snuggling down beneath coat and scarf, I knew that if I put dark glasses on to hide some bruises I would look ridiculous. I thought of Kolya on his way to Heathrow and imagined him getting back to his Tribeca apartment, all wooden floors and books and comfortable sofas.

Part of me wished I'd gone with him. I'd resisted his pleas to do so, sure that it would be better for me to process what had happened at home in my own space, but in some ways, I wished I was there, curled up and safe.

As the train crawled into York station, I saw a couple of cops on the platform and wondered again whether I should have told the police everything that had happened, instead of brushing it off as a mugging and telling them I had nothing of use to tell them. After all, without witnesses or physical evidence, there would be little for the police to go on. They'd already checked for CCTV footage of the mews where I'd been assaulted, but had come up empty-handed. My instinct was that Sokolov was a problem I needed to deal with myself.

Considering the nature of my job, I'd made very few enemies. Sure, there were undoubtedly some who held a grudge, but the bad guys I came into contact with generally accepted that recovering stolen art was a business transaction and I'd never experienced or seen much violence, the previous week's trip to St Petersburg excepted.

Then again, I rarely went round telling people that their multi-million dollar painting was a worthless fake.

Evidently that created a new breed of enemy, one who took that sort of thing personally. With hindsight, I should have expected Sokolov to lash out.

If he didn't know the Rothko was a forgery until I'd spotted it, why didn't he go after the hapless individual who'd sold it to him? Attacking me only reinforced my suspicion he'd known it was dodgy and hoped to pull a fast one.

His response was probably more extreme because I'd outwitted him more than once—by spotting that the Rothko wasn't right, refusing to track down the original, and finally, by outbidding him for the Picasso. Mind you, I wouldn't have been surprised if he'd only bid on that in order to try to exert his dominance over me. I'd dented his fragile ego twice in as many days and it was depressingly predictable that he would want to put me in my place. That he'd responded with such violence was chilling.

I was jolted from these thoughts by a video call. Forgetting my bruises, I answered and came face-to-face with Jason's beaming all-American good looks.

"Hey, Kate. I just wanted to say hi and how much I'm looking forward to the Picasso arriving—shit! What happened to you?" Clearly, the bruising to my face wasn't going down as fast as I hoped.

"It's fine. Just a mugger. Wrong time, wrong place." I forced a smile, jaw muscles aching from the effort as I tried to brush it off.

"If you say so." He didn't sound convinced.

"I'll chase Carlyle's tomorrow and see if they have an update."

"How do you feel?" Jason didn't seem willing to be distracted by business. "Are you resting? That looks real nasty."

"It feels nasty, but I'll be okay in a few days."

"You need a holiday, some Californian sun. Why don't you come out here? You could stay at the Big Sur house if you like. It's so peaceful there. Say yes, and I'll have tickets, or my plane, waiting for you wherever you need it."

"I'm sure it is, Jason, but I'll be fine. I'm on the train back home to Edinburgh and I just want to curl up there." I made an excuse and hung up. Looking out of the window at the drizzle, I had some second thoughts. A few days alone watching whales in the Pacific from Jason's deck sounded pretty perfect.

"Can you wait until I'm inside please?" The cabbie rolled his eyes. Despite the brooding sky, it was Sunday afternoon and Great King Street was as far from a rough neighbourhood as you could get. All the same, he loitered for the two minutes it took me to haul my luggage into the building and click the lock behind me. He'd been peering at me in the rear-view mirror during the short journey from the station but my injuries clearly didn't warrant him getting out in the drizzle to help me with my bags. I wished I hadn't tipped him.

Upstairs, my flat was as lovely as ever, the pale walls and oak parquet soothing to my soul. I'd warned Flora that I'd be back and wasn't feeling great. Going through to the kitchen to put the kettle on, I saw that she'd left me a casserole for supper in the fridge. Arthur appeared, glared at me, and sat down beside his food bowl, claiming that he couldn't possibly eat the perfectly fresh kibble Flora had given him earlier. I moved to pat him and he hissed, so I left him to it.

In the drawing room, I lit some lamps and put a match

to the logs in the grate. Going through to the study, I flicked through the mail Flora had piled on my desk. There wasn't anything that couldn't wait until I felt stronger.

But I couldn't settle. Nothing had been moved as far as I could see and nothing seemed to be missing, but there was a niggle at the back of mind. A disturbance in the atmosphere, almost.

Checking the alarm panel in the hall, I saw that it had been triggered twice. Returning to the office, I logged into the security company's website and saw that on both occasions they'd called and Flora had given the password. False alarms. It had gone off the previous evening, once at about seven pm, again at midnight.

That surprised me. I sometimes had pretty valuable artworks at home. Just temporarily and not Picasso level, but worth half the price of the flat and at my insurer's insistence, my alarm was high-spec, monitored, serviced regularly, and not given to going off for no reason. Certainly not twice in one night when the flat was empty. Arthur wouldn't have tripped it; I'd spent a small fortune having one installed that the furry fiend wouldn't set off.

I texted Flora:

"Thanks for putting dinner in the fridge. I owe you. The alarm panel says there were some false alarms. Any problems?"

She replied immediately:

"It was weird. Hang on, I'll be down in a minute."

I opened the door into the hallway so that she could just walk in, picked up my case and headed for my bedroom, planning to unpack and get a load of laundry on.

And that's where I found the disturbance in the atmosphere.

21

The air was heady with a sickly mixture of fragrance, the bottles swept off my chest of drawers along with framed photographs that had been smashed underfoot. Turning, I saw that the duvet had been stripped from my bed and the mattress slashed, pillows stabbed and spilling feathers. Cutting through the perfume was another smell—bleach, splashed over my bedlinen and rugs.

Shredded too, was the upholstery on the little Georgian sofa in front of the window. The glass in all the pictures was smashed and, heartbreakingly, the Matisse sketch that had been a gift from Kolya had been dashed to the floor, its frame in pieces and the fragile paper torn by jagged shards.

Heart racing, hearing Flora clattering down the stone stairs from her flat, I went out to the hall, a need to see the rest of the damage fighting with fear and a desire to protect her from who knew what.

"Christ!" She stopped dead in the doorway. "Kate, what happened to your face?"

"It doesn't matter." I waved a hand, dismissing my

injuries as old news. "I've found out what tripped the alarm. It's the bedroom."

"What?" She stepped past me and I reached out, too slowly to catch her arm and stop her and she swore as she looked at the devastation. "I'm sorry. I didn't realise." Flora turned back to me, her face stricken. "The door was closed so I was certain Arthur hadn't been in there. I thought he'd found a way to trigger the alarm. We should get out, what if they're still here?"

"They'll be long gone, Flora. And don't look so worried, it's not your fault." I reached out to squeeze her shaking hand. "I need to call the police."

While we waited, although I knew that I shouldn't contaminate any forensic evidence, the desire to see the full extent of the vandalism was stronger. I went back into my bedroom, stepping carefully over the glass, wincing as I saw that the huge old foxed mirror that faced my bed had been shattered.

In my dressing room things were worse, jewellery and makeup crushed underfoot as my wardrobes were emptied, more bleach thrown around. I picked up an Erdem dress, shredded like most of the rest. Drawers had been pulled open, the contents rifled. Whoever did this had even been through my underwear, silk and lace ripped to pieces. My shoes were chucked into the chaos, the heels snapped off some.

My hands were shaking as I tried to comprehend the damage. This destruction in my bedroom, where I slept, where I was at my most vulnerable, chilled me. They'd taken nothing. No, this was to remind me that it wasn't over simply because I'd retreated to Scotland. How far would I have to go before I was safe from Yuri Sokolov?

"Well, it could be worse." PC Forsyth took the cup of tea Flora handed her and sat down opposite me at the kitchen table.

"I suppose so. At least they didn't touch the rest of the flat." I was still cold and shocked, struggling to remind myself of the positive aspects of this.

"And it doesn't look as if they used your bedroom as a bathroom or left any, well, DNA deposits on your underwear."

"DNA? Oh—" Flora's voice trailed away, "That's disgusting."

"People who do this often are." Forsyth shrugged as though she'd seen too much to have any illusions left about human nature. "You're sure nothing was taken?"

"I won't know until I can start sorting everything out, but it doesn't look like it. My jewellery's still there. If they didn't take that, then they probably wouldn't bother with the rest."

"It seems very targeted, to break in just to vandalise your bedroom. Can you think of anyone who has a grudge? I see from our intelligence that you had difficulties with someone called Chris Hammond? There's a restraining order and he did serve a sentence for assault."

The police officer's eyes flitted over the bruises on my face. For a moment, I remembered the only other time I'd been injured like this and Chris' ongoing campaign of anonymous emails, but dismissed that thought. He wasn't responsible for this. He might send emails but he was too much of a coward to come near me again. At least, that's what I hoped.

"I'm not sure who broke in, but it won't have been Chris." I gesticulated toward my black eye. "This was a result of a mugging in London last week." I had kept my thoughts to myself, knowing that no-one would be able to hang anything on Sokolov or his heavies for the attack on me, but this was taking it to a new level. I'd assumed that Sokolov would see my retreat to Edinburgh as waving a white flag, that he'd back off thinking I'd learnt my lesson. But instead he wanted me to know that I wasn't even safe in my own home.

While I processed this, Flora and PC Forsyth ran through the events of the night before when the alarm had gone off. The most logical theory was that the intruders had broken in by picking the locks, careful not to damage the door so that when Flora came down, she'd suspect nothing and assume it was simply a glitch, and not realise that someone was hiding in the flat.

When they'd finished trashing my bedroom, they'd left, leaving the door just on the Yale lock. By the time the alarm triggered again, they would have been out of the main door at the bottom of the stairs and away down the street by the time Flora got back downstairs to my flat. That was the theory at any rate, and no-one had a better one.

"And you heard nothing? Despite being upstairs?"

"Not a thing. I had music on, although not especially loudly. All this must have happened during the evening, before I went to bed and these old buildings are pretty solid. Noise doesn't really travel. And Kate's bedroom is under mine, so if I'd been in the kitchen or the sitting room I'd have been even less likely to hear anything." Flora looked at me, apologetic. "I'm sorry, Kate."

"Don't be." I shook my head. "I'm glad you didn't hear anything. They weren't people you'd want to confront."

"I'll talk to the downstairs neighbours and the residents of the top flat. Maybe they saw something," PC Forsyth said.

"Perhaps. But the Hendersons downstairs are old and a bit deaf and I'm fairly sure James and Fiona upstairs were away. Perhaps someone in one of the other buildings will have noticed people hanging around?" Flora sounded hopeful, but I doubted that Sokolov's men would have been careless enough to be spotted.

Realising that whoever had done this had been hiding in the flat when Flora came downstairs after the first alarm chilled me. They wouldn't have shown her any mercy. I saw that dawn on her and she paled. So far, she hadn't joined up the dots and realised that my bruises and this break-in were related. That could wait, at least until the police left.

They did, soon after, assuring me that people would be round in the morning to take fingerprints, giving me a reference number for my insurers and reminders to lock up carefully.

"Come on." Flora squeezed my hand. "The spare bed's already made up. Have a hot bath to stop you shivering and I'll get dinner on."

Lying in the steaming bath, hoping that the potions Flora had added would live up to their calming and restorative claims, I felt the heat sink into my bones, easing away the cold shivers of fear and shock. The glass of wine she'd placed beside me was helping too. There, enveloped in peace and warmth, I contemplated the practical consequences of the break-in.

It looked as if the only clothes I now possessed were the ones I'd taken to London. Even if I could salvage anything, it would feel sullied and I'd probably send it to the local charity shop. Not that the clothes mattered; I could replace them. But the personal items, such as the Rodin sketch and the mirror I'd had shipped from a Venetian antique dealer, were irreplaceable. And I needed a mattress, bed linen, new curtains, an upholsterer—the list went on.

My phone rang in the hall and I called to Flora asking her to answer it, not yet ready to leave my cocoon of warmth. When I did get out I would have to call my insurers. That could definitely wait until I'd finished this glass of wine.

"Hi Pete, it's Flora. Kate can't come to the phone at the moment." I could hear her clearly. "She's here at my flat, in the bath." A pause. "No, she's fine. Not hurt, at any rate. No more than she was when she got here." I closed my eyes, wanting Flora to explain, to not have to go through it myself. "Her flat was broken into last night." Another pause. "No, I don't think they took anything, but they ransacked her bedroom." A silence, presumably while Pete asked more questions. "Look, you need to let Kate tell you about it. But she's okay and she's going to be staying here for a few nights, I think." A short pause. "I promise, Pete. I'll get her to call you as soon as she's out of the bath. But try not to worry." Another gap and then she said goodbye.

"That was Pete," Flora called through the door.

"So I gathered."

"He wants you to ring him straightaway. He sounded worried."

"Yes, I picked that up too." I slid under the water to rinse my hair and summoned the energy to return to the chaos that my life had become.

. . .

"Hi there." I decided that bright and breezy might be the best way to put Pete's mind at rest. "How's it going with you?"

"Flora told me you were burgled." To the point, that was Pete all over.

"Ah, yes, but it's fine. Only a bit of cleaning to do." I settled on Flora's sofa with another glass of wine.

"She used the word *ransacked*. That doesn't sound like you just need to tidy up. What's happened, Kate?" Pete's voice was warm and concerned rather than impatient as he'd been after the assault. I felt tears spring to my eyes—sympathy was never good when I was already struggling to keep it together.

"Someone broke in yesterday evening. They didn't touch anything except my bedroom and dressing room."

"Much damage?"

"Well..." I hesitated for a moment and then described the chaos—the clothes, the mirror, my bed, the pictures, the bleach. "They even tore up my underwear."

"Thank goodness you weren't home. It was Sokolov, right, no question about that?"

"I doubt there will be any evidence to link him to it, but I can't think of anyone else. Nothing was taken, so it definitely wasn't the usual type of burglars. In a way, it's good. I've been waiting for the other shoe to drop and now it has. I can get on with repairing the damage and move on. Sokolov's made his point."

"For the moment."

"This is it. Surely he'll let it go after this?" I'd been rationalising and didn't want Pete to dispel the comfort I'd created for myself.

"I hope so. But I reckon he's enjoying this, so don't underestimate him. You're staying with Flora?"

"For a day or two. I need to get the locks changed and clear up and buy a new mattress and so on. I don't really want to be alone right now."

"I can imagine. Where's Kolya?"

"New York."

"Have you told him about this?"

"No. I probably won't. He'll just try to persuade me to get on a plane and that doesn't resolve anything, does it?"

"I suppose not." Pete's quietness was striking. After our last conversation when he'd been so furious, I'd expected more of the same. "I wish I could get away and come to Edinburgh but I can't. I'm sorry."

"It's okay. That's not your job any more, Pete. And I really don't want to have to explain to Kolya that you're staying in my spare bedroom. I don't think he'd take that well." I smiled. "And what would you do? Carry my bags while I go into town to replace my wardrobe? Surely you don't want to come shoe shopping with me?"

"Maybe not. Happy to accompany you underwear shopping, though." He laughed, low and warm and reassuring. It was good to hear and made me smile despite myself. "But you're probably right. Call me if you need anything. I'll ring tomorrow."

"Okay. Thanks."

"Take care." He hung up and I sat for a moment, feeling a little better and hearing Flora moving about in the kitchen. I had good friends, for that I was very grateful.

22

By lunchtime the next day, what felt like half of Edinburgh had tramped through my flat and I was finally left alone to bag up the debris that I would have to throw out. A locksmith had been and replaced my locks with vastly expensive new ones that he said would be impregnable. The loss adjuster was understanding, just wanting a list and photographs so that her employers would know that I wasn't trying to inflate my claim. She crunched across the broken glass, shook her head at the bleach splattered everywhere and visibly winced at the sight of my bed, springs and wadding spilling from its wounds.

Finally, everyone left and there was no-one to look questioningly at my injuries or gape in horror at the damage in my flat. I was still uncomfortable though and started packing a few things to take upstairs to Flora's. I could have moved into my guest bedroom, but I knew I wouldn't settle there. It would be a few days before I felt safe enough to sleep alone in my flat.

About four, the doorbell rang and for a moment I panicked, wondering if the intruders had returned.

Reminding myself that it wasn't likely, I looked through the spyhole. There I saw two people—a middle-aged woman, a younger man, tired-looking, suits. Even through the tiny lens, I could tell they were cops. I sighed. More questions, no doubt. Or maybe they were here to assure me that they would find the men who'd broken in?

"Hi. How can I help?" I swung the door open and smiled, polite rather than welcoming.

"Good afternoon." The female officer spoke as they held up their Police Scotland warrant cards. They exchanged a glance and I realised that this wasn't a run-of-the-mill visit. "I'm DI Spencer and this is DC Crieff. We'd like to talk to Miss Kate Carpenter."

"I'm Kate. Is this about the burglary?"

"Please, may we come in?" I stepped back, opening the door wider and inviting them into the hall. I wanted to be helpful, but I'd seen enough of the police over the last few days. If this was to do with the burglary, surely they could have just phoned me? I looked at them and smiled, waiting.

"I believe you reported your bank cards missing after a mugging last week?"

"Yes. They took my wallet—cards, driving licence, all the usual." It baffled me. Why were Scottish CID officers here about a credit card lost in London? And then fear started to crawl down my neck. "What's happened?"

"Could you show us some identification, please?" DI Spencer's face still wasn't giving anything away. I hurried into my office and grabbed one of my passports from my desk drawer. She checked it, squinting at the photograph and handed it to DC Crieff, who jotted some details down.

"Why are you here? This seems excessive for a lost Amex card." I could feel my shoulders tensing, my pulse beating a little faster.

"Your cards have been recovered in Edinburgh." Both cops still looked far too serious for something this trivial.

"Right. Thanks for letting me know. But you could have just called." I smiled, not wanting to sound unfriendly.

"We needed to check you were safe. And we're going to need a more detailed statement about how your cards were taken than you gave to the Met in London after the mugging."

"What aren't you telling me?" I knew there was something, it was in their cautious manner, the looks they exchanged. "Where did you find them?"

"We found the body of a woman near the docks in Leith and the death appears non-accidental. Your cards were on the body. Given the circumstances, we needed to make sure you were safe..." Her voice tailed off as I sprinted to the bathroom, vomit rising in my throat.

Leaning on the washbasin, I wiped the cold sweat from my brow as I waited for the nausea to pass. A thousand thoughts ran through my head, the coincidences of a corpse with my identification, ID that had been taken by an attacker who'd undoubtedly assaulted me on Sokolov's orders. And she'd been found in my city, a couple of days after my flat was trashed. I took a few deep breaths, trying to stop my heart racing.

I returned to the police officers waiting in the hall and tried to look more together. I could take most things in my stride but it seemed that after the last week, I'd run out of that ability. DI Spencer introduced herself as Rebecca and put a hand on my arm, her eyes flicking around my face as she looked at my bruises.

"I'm sorry. It looks like you've had a tough few days."

"You could say that. Come on, I need a cup of tea." Leading them through to the kitchen, I put the kettle on and sat down at the table. DC Crieff, John, took over the tea-making with the practised air of someone used to being the bearer of bad news.

"I think you'd better start at the beginning," I suggested. "I'm Kate Carpenter and I'm very much alive despite the black eye."

"So I see." Rebecca looked apologetic. She was still holding my passport, and she leafed through it again and put it to one side. "As I said, a body was found and the only ID was a wallet containing various items with your name. Here are some photographs." She passed across an iPad and I flicked through the images—my bank cards, gym entry pass, a couple of loyalty cards, museum memberships, and so on—all things that had been taken from my bag by Sokolov's thug after he assaulted me. I handed it back.

"Are those yours?"

"Yes. My wallet was stolen in London last week. There was also ID with my photo on, was that found on her? My driving licence and so on."

"No, just these."

"My wallet was in her pocket?" The officers exchanged another look.

"No. The purse was in a handbag tied around her neck. It looked as though she'd been strangled with the strap."

"I see." The nausea rose again and DC Crieff moved fast to put a glass of water in front of me. "The photo ID wasn't there because you were supposed to think it was me," I said quietly.

"It's more likely that the dead woman found your purse and ditched the photo ID as it was of no use to her. She'd have kept the bank cards if she thought she could use them, contactless payments and so on. There was also a fair amount of heroin in her system. Drugs might have been the motivation for the assault on you." I could understand why that might seem a more probable explanation, but I knew I was right. "Presumably, you sustained those injuries during your mugging?"

"Yes." I explained some of what happened, skipping over the fact that I knew who'd assaulted me, reassuring her that it wasn't a domestic incident, just a straightforward mugging and that I didn't get a good look at my attacker.

"I see." DI Spencer made a note. I didn't think she completely believed me but I'd lied about this supposed mugging so often that it came easily to me now. "So it definitely couldn't have been a woman who attacked you? Maybe the dead woman?"

"No. It was a man who did this. It would have been a fairer fight with a woman and I don't think a drug addict would have had the chance to do this much damage." I took a gulp of water and a thought struck me. "What did the woman look like?" I asked, nausea replaced by a creeping sense of dread.

"The pathologist's report described her as very slim, tall, early twenties, bleached hair, probably Eastern European," DI Spencer said, referring to her iPad. "Do you think she might have been involved in the mugging? An accomplice maybe?"

"Did she have bruising on the side of her face?" Please, I thought, please tell me it couldn't have been the woman I saw in Sokolov's house and at the park, the woman I should have helped but didn't. The two cops exchanged a look.

"The deceased woman sustained a number of injuries." She looked at the screen and paused. "There were some broken ribs, bruising to her face, cigarette burns to her body, ligature marks to her wrists. And signs of sexual assault. The pathologist thought the bruises on her face were older injuries, maybe a week or so."

"Do you know who she was?" I swallowed hard and took a mouthful of tea.

"We don't. No DNA or fingerprints on record, and her dentistry was foreign. We may find out via other agencies but at the moment we have little to go on. If you'd be willing to look I could show you a picture of her face? Maybe you'll recognise her."

I nodded. I didn't want to see her, but I owed it to whoever that woman was. It may be that she was a stranger who'd simply found my wallet chucked to one side. But if it was the woman I'd seen and failed to help, what then? DI Spencer pulled up another photograph and slid the tablet across the table.

Lying there in the mortuary, as I'd feared, with eyes closed and skin waxy pale, was the girl from Sokolov's hallway. I recognised her by the bruises that covered the side of her face, just like my own. Only there were more now. And even dead, she had the same hopeless expression as when I'd seen her in Sokolov's house.

Light-headed, I took a few mouthfuls of the tea that Crieff had had the foresight to add sugar to. A sense of self-preservation reminded me that I'd had a lucky escape.

Then guilt came crashing in, screaming that I should have helped her, should have insisted that she come with me to a police station, not put it on a mental back-burner and let my inaction allow this to happen.

And then came the fear. Cold, skin-crawling, stomach-twisting terror. I'd thought that the assault in the mews was a punishment, the drawing of a line, and that the destruction in my flat was simply underlining that.

But Sokolov had clearly decided even that wasn't enough to make his point and so he did this. Or, almost certainly, had his henchmen do this. The tragedy that resulted in this young woman with no name ending up on a pathologist's slab was terrible. That they'd killed her just to persecute me was horrific. That my identification was found on her was a warning that chilled me.

I drank more tea, spilling some on the table with shaking hands. Crieff and Spencer looked expectant, seeing that this was far more than a reaction to the sight of that girl's corpse.

"Kate, are you all right?" Crieff's voice was low, full of concern.

"Do you know who she is?" DI Spencer leaned forward, sensing that I might have information. I tried to pull myself together as best I could. Should I tell her? And how much should I tell her? I looked again at the photograph and knew that I had to give her all the information that I could.

"I don't know her name," I began, "but I first saw her in London a week or so ago. I'm an art advisor and I do some security consulting for insurance brokers as well. I went to a property from which a valuable painting had been taken and she was there. I saw the bruises on her face. Then she was pulled away, out of sight, by one of the homeowner's bodyguards, I saw that she was afraid. But I was preoccupied, and did nothing." I hung my head, staring into my mug of tea. "She was in the park with the same bodyguard a couple of days later and I tried to talk to her, but he hustled her into a car and I let it go. I didn't do anything to help."

"We could have done something if you'd informed the police at the time." Crieff's tone was annoyed, the idealism of the young. I shook my head.

"No. I don't think you could. It was Yuri Sokolov's house.

His money and his lawyers mean that these things never stick. You haven't managed to pin anything on him before. You'd have gone to the house and been told to come back with a warrant and by the time you did, she'd have gone. Assuming you could even get a warrant based on my say-so." Despair washed over me and I closed my eyes. DC Crieff could be as idealistic as he liked, but I knew how this worked and the look on DI Spencer's face showed that she did too.

Crieff and Spencer left about six having taken a statement. It wasn't a long one; I couldn't tell them much. By now, there wouldn't be any evidence left at Sokolov's house and the man who'd actually snuffed out the dead woman's life—because she was disposable and more useful as a warning to me than as a living, breathing person—would be long gone. My attacker hadn't spoken, but I guessed he was foreign, recruited from wherever Sokolov found his tame thugs. He'd disappear into some underworld with a new story and a new name and who knew what his ultimate fate might be. But no-one would hold him responsible for this.

After the police had gone, I locked the front door behind them and took a deep breath. I would regret my inaction for the rest of my life and I'd never let anything like this happen again. But it was a savage way to learn that lesson.

23

The sun was rising as I started to run, jogging slowly at first as I felt muscles still aching from the fight, begin to stretch again. Gradually, I settled into something approaching my usual pace, maybe a little tentative, although that was as much due to the bruises on my backside as the nervous desire to keep looking over my shoulder. But after two or three miles, I was moving more or less normally and enjoying the speed and agility that came with it.

In St Andrew's Square, I stopped and bought a takeaway coffee, sitting on one of the stone benches and gazing into the inky blackness of the reflecting pool. I'd barely slept the night before. Every time I closed my eyes I saw the face of the dead woman as she lay in the mortuary, bleak and beaten.

When I'd been assaulted by Chris, I'd had people to help me. She'd had no-one and I could have helped her, but didn't. The guilt hit me in waves that almost knocked me off my feet. As did the fear.

I couldn't help but wonder where the next blow would

come from. Were my friends safe? What if Sokolov sent someone to attack Flora or Kolya or Joe? Or would he come after me again?

I looked around the square, at the people cutting through on their way to work, the tourists strolling in the early morning sunshine, and remembered the St Petersburg park only a couple of weeks earlier and a man shot in the back of the head by an assassin he never saw coming. My shoulders tensed as I fought the desire to look round, to see if any of these passers-by had been sent with another, more final message.

Naively, I'd assumed sending his tame thug to beat me up would be enough for Sokolov, lashing out in a fit of temper that would burn itself out once he knew he'd made his point.

The ransacking of my bedroom was excessive but after finding the destruction I'd rationalised that he'd be satisfied now with two attacks, tallying with the two occasions where he felt I'd crossed him—spotting the dodgy Rothko and then outbidding him at the auction. I hoped he'd think that we were square, and that I could get back to my life and bide my time as I waited for a chance to exact retribution of my own.

But with news of the dead woman, I realised these attacks of Sokolov's were nothing to do with repaying me for perceived slights. Rather, he simply liked to hurt people and had no empathy to tell him enough was enough. Whether he was a psychopath or sociopath was immaterial. What I did know was that he wouldn't give up easily. He would continue to torment me for as long as it amused him and even if he backed off for a while, it would be impossible to predict when and how he might next lash out.

Draining my coffee cup, I threw it in a nearby bin and

started to walk home. If Sokolov wouldn't back off of his own volition, I would have to find his weakness and use that to force him into submission.

Back in my office, breaking off from deleting most of my in-box, I answered my phone.

"Hi, Joe. How's it going?"

"It's Sokolov, Kate." He sounded different, not stressed as usual but agitated. "Ellie's just called me. She's in quite a state."

"What's happened?" I swung round in my chair, glancing out of the window as though fearing that mention of him would conjure one of his henchmen outside my house.

"She was in the supermarket earlier and noticed some bloke who seemed to be following her. You know the sort of thing I mean. He was too close, too often. Ellie's not easily phased so she thought he was just some random weirdo, but then she was at the park with the kids after school and he was there, just stood watching them."

"That's not good."

"No. And then when she got home and was getting the girls out of the car, she saw him drive past the house."

I swore under my breath. In some ways, it was predictable that Sokolov would turn his attentions to my wider circle, especially Joe, who had, after all, employed me to look into the theft of the Rothko. And it was equally predictable that he would go after Joe's weak spot—his wife and children. Joe had seen my injuries when they were raw and still bleeding, and I'd told him about the break-in, but I hadn't informed him about the dead woman. That wasn't going to help him feel any less worried.

"Ring Pete. He's been threatening me with a minder so tell him you need someone to keep an eye on Ellie and the girls. He'll know someone that he can despatch to your place." Ellie was Pete's cousin, he'd have a former comrade there by dinnertime.

"You really think that's necessary?"

"I think it's wise to be cautious."

"Okay." He sounded a little calmer. "What's it come to, Kate? That we need to live like this? I work in insurance, for fuck's sake. And if I go to the police, what do I say? They can't do anything, can they?"

"No. Well, they'll probably log it and see if a pattern emerges, I suppose, but that's not much use." I sighed, my head heavy. "Call Pete, now. And I'll ring you later. I need to think of a plan, a way to get Sokolov off our backs."

"What sort of plan?" Joe asked, wary.

"I don't know yet. But I'll come up with something, I promise. Now, go and ring Pete."

Flora was at a parents' evening that night, three hours of telling parents that their children would only get better at their instruments if they practised, and trying to let others down, gently explaining that they would not live their own Festival Hall dreams via their tone-deaf offspring. She was a good friend, but her worried concern for me was making me edgy and so I enjoyed the quiet while I attempted to unravel my thoughts, curled up on her sofa with a takeaway and a glass of wine.

When my phone rang and Kolya's face flashed up, I rolled my eyes. Not answering was tempting, but I'd already let three or four of his calls go to voicemail in the last couple of days, sending cheerful texts instead about how I was catching up with work and I'd get back to him just as soon as I had a spare minute. I hadn't told him about the break-in or the dead woman and didn't plan to.

"Hello, my darling." Even the flickering connection of the Face Time call couldn't dim those cornflower eyes or that smile.

"Hi." I shifted on the sofa, getting more comfortable, trying to appear as though I was taking it easy.

"How do you feel? Your bruises look a little better."

"I'm feeling okay. Just sleeping a lot and getting back to work. I'll be completely back on form in a few days."

"Good." I saw his eyes flicker around the screen. "Where are you? That doesn't look like your flat."

"I'm at Flora's. She's making dinner."

"How kind. Give her my best wishes."

"I will." I fidgeted, aware that this small talk was unlike our usual easy conversation. I wanted to tell him everything but at the same time, I knew that his reaction wouldn't help. He'd try to order me onto a plane to New York, his intentions well-meant but smothering. "What are you up to? It's mid-afternoon, isn't it?"

"Yes. I was tired so I took the afternoon off. I've lit a fire, I'm cooking dinner, listening to music, and I'm going to have an early night to see if I can shake off my jet-lag."

"That sounds lovely." I could imagine his open-plan apartment, warm with lamplight and the glow of the fire, a Rachmaninov piano concerto playing. I saw us sitting at the kitchen island sharing a meal and a bottle of wine, curled up in front of a movie, or reading in companionable silence.

"You could be here. If you would only get on a plane, you could be here for breakfast. You don't even need to pack; you have clothes here and in case you'd forgotten, we do have shops in New York. Just take your passport, go to the airport, and buy a seat on the next flight here." He smiled. "You make life hard for yourself, you know that?"

"I know. But there are things here to be settled first. Things I need to do."

"Like the Robert Frost poem."

"Eh?"

"Stopping by Woods. The last line is *'but I have promises to keep and miles to go before I sleep.'*"

"Of course. Yes, I have a couple of promises to keep." I didn't want to tell him that the last line of the poem was often interpreted as an analogy for death. Again, the dead woman's face flashed before my eyes.

"To do with Sokolov?"

"Kind of. Now more than ever. But I'll make sure I stay safe, trust me."

"I wish you were here, Kate. Or that I was with you. If only you'd move to New York. You would be away from Sokolov and all that stress and we'd have more time for each other."

"I know. Give me time to keep this promise and then we'll see what I can do." I smiled, hoping it didn't look forced, biting back all the words I knew I needed to say. Kolya smiled back, his face full of affection and warmth and I felt a wave of sadness, knowing that I would hurt him when I told him that I couldn't share the future he saw for us. But that could wait. First, I had other things to deal with.

Lying in bed, the problem of what to do about Yuri Sokolov ran round and round my mind. I'd said to Kolya that I had promises to keep and it was true. Promises to myself and to Joe, but most of all to the dead woman in the morgue with no name and no-one to mourn her. Yet again, I found myself wishing I'd done something other than let her slip from my mind to face such a grim end.

Giving up on sleep, I sat up and reached for my laptop, pulling up news stories about Sokolov, looking for a thread to pick at that would enable me to see how to deal with him. The interviews he gave were immaculately stage-managed, the persona of the businessman-turned-art-collector carefully crafted to hide his grubbier background.

But looking into the details skipped over in interviews but talked about on news sites and discussion forums, I found the truth of his origins. He'd had a poor childhood, made his fortune by being more ruthless than others, and used that money to buy his way into the upper echelons of society. He could have anything he wanted and what he wanted was respect.

I knew Sokolov was a vain man. From the omissions in those magazine profiles, I could tell that he was ashamed of his roots and that his now-lofty social position mattered desperately to him. He hadn't gone to the Eardisley Gallery party to socialise or to appreciate the art on display. He was there to show everyone, maybe even to convince himself, that he belonged in that world. That need was visceral, and because it was common knowledge now that he'd been conned over the Rothko, his ego was bruised. That was why he'd lashed out, his lack of empathy rendering him without any sense of proportion.

In Orwell's Room 101, Sokolov's nightmare would be the sound of people mocking him. But it wasn't just his ego I wanted to undermine. I would need to threaten his wealth, his business, even his freedom. I'd had enough of him thinking he could attack me, and it turned my stomach that he'd treated another woman as disposable merely to terrorise me. How many others were there? Perhaps I could ensure that no more women ended up dead because of him.

But I needed facts, not rumours or conjecture, to build a wall of evidence that would keep him at bay. I needed to wield enough power that he couldn't risk crossing me. I needed to find the dirt he'd tried so hard to hide, the secrets that could destroy him.

24

Abandoning any hope of sleep now that I had a plan forming in my mind, I made a cup of tea and went back to bed.

I wasn't entirely sure where Pete was. He and the guys he worked with had very specialised skill sets that were highly valued in areas where hostage rescue was sometimes necessary and news crews needed to be kept safe. Attributes that were less sought after in, say, Tunbridge Wells. Guessing he'd be in somewhere in the Middle East that would make it about seven am.

Pete was an early riser unless he had company, so chances were that I wouldn't wake him. I tapped his number and waited while thousands of exchanges and phone masts connected us. And his phone went straight to voicemail. Maybe he wasn't alone? I pushed away the emotions that brought up and went back to a Vanity Fair article about Sokolov the art connoisseur. Thirty seconds later, Pete called.

"Sorry, I was asleep. How's it going?"

"Fine. Sorry to disturb you."

"That's okay. I never mind you waking me up." I could tell he was smiling, heard him moving as though getting comfortable in bed and the softness of his breath. If I closed my eyes it was as though he were next to me. "What can I do for you?"

"Couple of things." I pulled myself together and tried to be brisk. "Firstly, did Joe get hold of you yesterday?"

"He did. And three hours later Sam arrived at his place. He won't let Ellie or the girls out of his sight."

"That's good." Sam was an ex-Marine, warm and funny with a deceptively easy-going manner. If Sokolov's thug caused trouble, Sam would be more than a match for him.

"It's worrying that Sokolov's ramping things up."

"He's pushing it further than I would have expected," I said. "The police were here the day before yesterday. They found a body by the docks in Leith with my ID on her." I closed my eyes, trying to push away the memory of the photograph as I explained, close to tears but determined not to let my voice so much as quiver. When I'd finished, Pete was quiet for a few moments.

"And all this because you told him his painting was a forgery?"

"A very expensive one, but yes, that's what started this. Now it's just about him getting a kick out of tormenting people. He's a sadist. That poor woman. And he knows I'm scared and he's enjoying it."

"Bastard. Be careful. Please, can I—"

"No." I knew what he would say.

"I've been asking around. Everyone seems to have a story about something they've heard. I'll try to get back to the UK next week."

"Don't do that. I'll be okay." I tried to sound convincing. "But I need a favour."

"Anything."

"I have to find proof of those stories about him. He'll toy with me and with Ellie too, for as long as it amuses him, but to make him retreat, I need ammunition. Do you have someone on your team who could spare me a few hours to see what they can dig up? I want the stuff that isn't public knowledge. But it has to be solid, not rumours. If I have to put this in front of him I need him to be scared witless because I know all his secrets."

"Sure. I'll call a friend. She works in IT for one of the military contractors in Hereford. Becky can get into pretty much anywhere."

"Thanks." I felt more positive already now that I was starting to get a plan in place. "And quickly please, I don't want him escalating things with Joe and his family."

"I'll ring her this morning. Maybe let her have her breakfast first?"

"Okay, I suppose."

"And how are your injuries? Healing okay?"

"My face is less swollen and my bruises are fading. You can hardly see the shape of his fist in the one on my abdomen any more." I tried to sound breezy. "I'll send you a picture."

"Not the sort of picture of you I'd like to see." Pete's tone was warm now, teasing me.

"Yes, well, that's not happening."

"A man can dream."

"You'll have to keep dreaming." I hesitated. "Anyway, I'll let you get on. Thanks."

"Any time. Bye. I—" A pause. "Bye." And he was gone.

I felt better for having spoken to Pete, calmer and more focussed. Smiling, remembering his comments about my injuries, I flicked around on my phone and sent three that

I'd taken just after the attack. When I compared them to what I saw in the mirror now, I was pleased to see how much they'd faded.

The ones I sent were pretty raw though; the bruise on my stomach and the side of my face. I also took a snap of my cheek, to prove how much my bruises had faded. I was so used to it by now that I didn't think how shocking those images might be, even to Pete who'd seen all kinds of unimaginable horrors. I suppose it's different when it's someone you care about. His response came in a couple of minutes:

"Are you sure I can't just have him killed? That would put a stop to this for certain."

I smiled. I had a plan, but it was nice to know that there were other options still open to me.

Although my main goal was to find the leverage that would ensure Sokolov backed off for good, the stolen Rothko kept niggling at the corners of my mind. I was interested for my own reasons and for anyone else I would have been on the trail of the original long ago. Finding the truth of the theft wasn't essential but I couldn't help but feel that I needed to know what happened, that it would be useful. After all, that painting was emblematic of Sokolov's desire to be accepted into cultured, polite society and his rage at the public exposure of it as a forgery was an insight into that deep-seated need. And I was nosy.

After I'd spoken to Pete, I gave up on sleep and went for a run, leaving a note for Flora so she wouldn't worry if she got up and found me gone. After about four miles of letting my mind wander over the facts I knew about the theft, something struck me.

Everyone moves in very individual ways that are determined by the manner in which they habitually use their bodies. Even just pushing a cart around the Tribeca branch of Whole Foods, Kolya moved like a dancer, forty-odd years of habit and muscle memory having created a grace and deliberateness that was unmistakable.

I had run all my life to some degree, and my style was smooth and efficient, no fuss. I ran for purpose, not effect, and I was careful not to waste energy or risk injury with poor technique, the odd unexpected pot-hole or lop-sided cobble notwithstanding. And people were recognisable from a distance simply by their walk. Sometimes if we saw a friend ahead of us in the street we knew who it was even if we couldn't see their faces.

I'd mentioned in an off-hand way that the Rothko thief must be some kind of gymnast to get away across the rooftops with a canvas like that over their shoulder and Kolya had joked that maybe it was a career open to him now that he danced a little less. I'd paid no attention then, the likelihood of a troupe of acrobats spending their free time looting modern art being pretty low. And besides, by then I was sure it was a fake, so I had lost interest. But something had been niggling me about that CCTV footage.

Back in my office, still in my running gear, I pulled up the file and let it play again and again, every flicker of the thief's movements familiar by now. They first appeared sprinting down the stairs and along the landing to the painting. And when they had bundled the canvas up, they ran back again with their awkward burden.

But that person didn't move like a runner. Rather they had the foot placement of a dancer. The picture was crappy quality and there was no chance of identifying them with that balaclava on, but movement was harder to disguise. I called Joe.

"Hi. How's your new house guest?"

"Sam? He's great. The kids love him and had him playing Minecraft with them yesterday evening. Ellie's less keen on having a minder but I reckon he'll win her over. We all slept a lot better last night, that's for sure. How are you?" The relief in Joe's voice was striking.

"Good. Much better this morning. I've got a plan for dealing with Sokolov."

"Don't poke a wasps nest, Kate." Joe sounded wary.

"It'll be fine. Trust me. There were some DNA traces at the crime scene that your guys collected. Do you have a match?"

"No. Frustratingly, it doesn't match up with what you got from de Bruin. And obviously, we don't have access to the police databases. Not that they've made any arrests, so I imagine they've got sweet FA too."

"Get a sample from the girlfriend, Olga," I said, going through to the kitchen to switch the kettle on.

"What? How?"

"That's your problem, not mine. Find someone to follow her. Do what I did with de Bruin. If people are off their guard, it's easy. And get a woman to do it, don't send one of your ex-cops after her. They'll arouse her suspicion."

"Are you going to tell me what this is about?"

"Later. But I think I know what happened to that painting."

I hung up and watched the footage again. Now that I had a theory about the thief, I could see so many little giveaways. Clearly, I was more attentive than Kolya gave me credit for when it came to dancing. I found his details on my phone and tapped the Face Time option.

"Hello, gorgeous." I grinned as he answered and then realised it would be half-four in the morning in New York. He managed a sleepy smile all the same.

"This is lovely. Early, but lovely all the same. How are you?"

"Sorry. Do you want me to call you back later?"

"No, it's fine." He rubbed his eyes and ran a hand through his hair. "I imagine it's important?"

"Kind of. It might mean that Sokolov gets payback."

"Kate, no." Kolya was wide awake now. "Enough of this. I won't have you putting yourself at risk again."

"I wasn't aware that it was up to you what I did." There was a warning note in my voice and I hoped he heard it. "Besides, it's not risky."

"Okay." He still looked wary but wisely gave up lecturing me.

"You remember how you and Olga, his girlfriend, kind of recognised each other?"

"Yes. But it was just a flicker. She's not that distinctive and my world is full of women. When I looked closer I didn't know her." He shrugged and I smiled.

"I need to know if she was a dancer. I have to find out where she knew you from. She may have changed her name, but if I email you some pictures and the few details I can find about her, will you ask around for me, please? Your company manager might remember her. Or Marcella." Both of those women were razor-sharp and I had a feeling they'd soon have the information I needed.

"Okay. Should I wake them, or can it wait until I get to the studio?" He raised an eyebrow.

"I think you should wait. They don't like me enough to be woken this early. I'm sorry again."

"It doesn't matter at all. I'm always pleased to see you.

Although I'd rather you were here, beside me. Now that would be worth waking at this hour for." He smiled, sleepy and seductive.

"Soon, darling. I've got to go. Speak later." I hung up, refusing to let myself dwell on my feelings about Kolya. That could wait.

Having set things in motion, I went out for a while, running some of the errands that would enable me to return home. It was time to stop hiding in Flora's flat, afraid of the threats that haunted my dreams and so I set off for John Lewis. Arriving home, new duvet and pillows under my arm and with a mattress due to be delivered in a few days, I checked my messages and called Joe back.

One of his investigators was married to a police officer on maternity leave, and she'd been persuaded to find a way of getting fingerprints and maybe even DNA from Olga. It wouldn't be obtained in the proper manner via a mouth swab and couldn't be used in court, but it might confirm a few things.

"But she could have handled that painting in the past. She's his bloody art advisor, she lives in the same house. I can't see what this will achieve, Kate." Joe sounded weary, worn out by the stress of Sokolov's fury. I knew that feeling.

"I know and I'm not sure either. But it feels like information I need, so trust me."

"I suppose." He sighed. "But if you're thinking she had something to do with the theft, what's her motive? What does she gain?"

"I think it's more to do with what she might lose."

I called Lucien, left him a voicemail and sent him an email to underline my point. I really needed to talk to him although given that I'd already twigged to his involvement with Olga, I could see why he'd prefer to avoid me.

Mid-afternoon, Kolya rang. It was late morning, New York time, so his staff must have come up with the goods pretty quickly. He was full of excitement about his work and some element of the new piece that was coming together. After a bit, when he paused for breath, and I asked if he had any information for me.

"Ah, yes. Olga Kovalenko, as she was known before she was Olga Yanovna."

"She changed her name?"

"Yes. Marcella recognised one of the pictures of her and managed to uncover some details. She's going to email you but I wanted to tell you first. I didn't want her stealing my glory."

The email from Marcella arrived shortly after, as concise as I'd expect. A formidable French woman in her late forties —neat dark bun, vintage Chanel and Dior, terrifyingly Parisian, she'd been Kolya's right hand for over a decade. She knew every detail of his life, arranged everything from doctors' appointments to contracts. As I'd pointed out the previous week, he was unaware of the lengths people went to in order to smooth his path. Marcella was one of the chief path-smoothers.

According to Marcella, Olga had moved to the USA from Siberia when she was about twelve. Her family wasn't wealthy, and she'd won several scholarships to enable her to go to ballet school in the States.

She'd auditioned for the New York Ballet Theatre three times when Kolya was artistic director there. Hence why she knew who Kolya was but he only vaguely recognised her. Apparently, Olga wasn't a bad dancer, but she was unlucky and each time she auditioned, there was always someone just a little better. At other times, on other days, she would have got in.

Marcella had made some calls and discovered that Olga had joined another, lesser, ballet company, had a couple of injuries, taken some time off and was modelling and working in an art gallery when she met Yuri Sokolov.

Looking at the images attached to the email, Olga had morphed from pretty, fresh-faced girl to the expensively elegant woman I'd seen in London practically overnight, shedding the persona of the ambitious young dancer just as quickly as she shed her old name. Yanovna was her middle, or patronymic, name. Like Sokolov, Olga Yanovna had risen almost without trace.

I had a contact, Clyde, in the States who I'd worked with in the past—a gallery in San Francisco had reason to be grateful to both of us—and so I fired off an email to him asking him to follow a few things up for me. I felt a hum of excitement. Vague and ill-formed as they were at the moment, my theories were starting to come together.

25

By late afternoon, I was feeling pleased with my day's work. I now knew Olga's origins and that she'd worked in a gallery in New York. I suspected that it would turn out to be the one where Sokolov had bought the dodgy Rothko. The paperwork relating to the sale was vague, to the extent that I'd raised an eyebrow back when the painting was taken and Joe sent me all the info he had on it.

Joe emailed too, his tone more cheerful than earlier now that he had a progress report for me. The wife of one of his investigators had, after spending the afternoon following Olga around central London department stores, managed to pull my trick, dropping her bag at her feet in Selfridges and handing her a water bottle while they both smiled and scooped up her spilled belongings.

Clearly, this was turning out to be a failsafe technique. Fingers crossed there would be decent fingerprints and maybe even enough touch DNA for a partial match, at least. I didn't need police-level evidence, just something to back up my gut feeling.

There was also an email from my American contact that simply read: *"Call me."* That sounded promising. Clyde wasn't chatty at the best of times so he must have something useful for me.

Before I could ring him, the phone rang. A withheld number; probably someone trying to scam me about a road accident I'd never had, I assumed.

"Hi."

"Is that Kate Carpenter?" The female voice was brisk and efficient.

"It is."

"This is Becky Curtis. Pete asked me to look into Yuri Sokolov for you."

"Brilliant. Thanks. How are you getting on?"

"It's going to take another day or so to get all the information. Security on some databases is tighter than others. But I'll get there. In the meantime, there's loads for you to be going on with."

"Brilliant." I was relieved. Hopefully this would give me the firepower I needed.

"I'd heard a bit about Sokolov, like you do, and I suspected his background must be fairly shady. Too much money to have come by it entirely ethically, you know?" Becky sounded as though she'd already spent too long digging through the grubbiness of Sokolov's life.

"Yes. I know what you mean."

"But there's all sorts out there. Mostly relating to protection money, dodgy business practices, trades union officials who've conveniently disappeared, convenient deaths of business rivals, people illegally evicted from property he wanted to redevelop."

"That's kind of what I expected."

"But I've found other stuff. Murdered women and girls

who filed complaints of being raped but then disappeared. Nothing specific yet, but I'll get there by tomorrow. I can stay here all night if I have to. You want all that?" Becky sounded doubtful, as though hesitant about sharing what sounded disturbing information.

"I do. I'm sorry."

"That's okay. It takes a lot to shock me but you should be careful. Pete told me what Sokolov did to you. And about the dead woman."

"She's why I need all this." I could hear the bleakness in my voice, aware now that she was just one of many victims. "I could have helped her, but I didn't."

"And you think you'll be able to use this to put him away?"

"Probably not given the time that's passed. You know, different jurisdictions and how I'm getting this information. But with luck, I can use it to make him think twice about doing it again."

"Good." There was a pause, as we both contemplated the brutal ends other women had suffered at his hands. "I'll be in touch."

"Thanks." I smiled. "You must owe Pete a heck of a favour."

"I owe him my life. Speak soon." And, without giving me time to ask questions, she was gone, leaving me feeling hollow and exhausted. Nothing Becky had told me was unexpected, but knowing and suspecting were different things. Knowing put me on a path I couldn't step off now.

I called Clyde.

"Hey. You've got some information? Tell me something to make me happy."

. . .

Clyde did indeed make me happy.

"Hey babe, I've got some info you're going to like." He started talking and I scribbled notes. Clyde had found the gallery Olga had worked at in New York, a gallery that had some problems with forged paintings and which had since closed down. As an ex-cop, he knew how to find the information I needed about the other forgeries and it should be with me in the next day or two.

"One more thing. I'm not sure it's possible, but if there were any fingerprints or DNA traces found in the evidence for that case, do you think you could get that info for me?"

"That might be pushing it, Kate," he laughed. "It's not as though I'm offering them the whereabouts of the Isabella Stewart Gardner haul in return."

"One day maybe." I'd love to find those paintings, and not just for the ten million dollar reward. "But I suspect there will be some prints they've never managed to match to any suspects and I think I know who they belong to."

"I'm sure the NYPD will be interested in that. I'll talk to one of my former colleagues, see what they've got."

"Thanks, Clyde."

I pulled up a picture of Olga Yanovna on my screen. It was taken just after she morphed into Sokolov's elegant girlfriend, no longer the struggling dancer but a glossy, high-maintenance accessory. I had a strong suspicion what she'd done and was certain the information arriving in my in-box would confirm it.

Next morning, after another restless night of little sleep and an early run to wake me up, I was showered and back at my desk by nine, ready to pick up the phone and carry on.

There were exciting elements of my art recovery work—an exchange in a busy foreign marketplace, lots of travel, that moment when all the strands of an investigation came together and I located a valuable piece, the adrenaline rush when I finally had the artwork in my hands. But most of my work, the donkey work that enabled that buzz, was done at my desk. Endless phone calls and conversations that gleaned a grain of information here or a rumour there. But eventually, I'd find the right person, or people, and the clue that would lead to my quarry.

I read the files that Clyde had sent over, smiling as I saw that I'd been right, and I called John Dixon, one of my art school lecturers and an expert on Mark Rothko's work. Now that Sokolov's painting had been proved to be a fake, something John told me he'd suspected since it first reappeared on the art scene, he was happy to spend a little time looking into the painting's history for me.

Specifically, I wanted to know how it had gone from hanging in the house pictured in the 1960s architecture book, to being rediscovered and sold to Yuri Sokolov.

Now that I'd worked out the scam, I was getting worried about Olga's safety. What Becky had found out hadn't been a surprise, just the confirmation of what I'd had an uneasy feeling about. But it meant that there was no way Sokolov would respond well when he found out what Olga had done and that must surely be soon, if he hadn't already joined the dots up. I called Lucien, left a message telling him to call me urgently, whatever time it was, and hoped he'd do so soon.

. . .

I also wanted to know how the painting had been transported around the world so I rang a shipping company, Harrisons, who worked for me regularly. In fact, the same people to whom I—or rather, Jason—was paying a small fortune to transport *Femme en Sommeil* to her new home in California. Finding their invoice in a sheaf of photocopies relating to the Rothko that Joe had sent me had been a sweet surprise.

When most of us moved house, we had to cross our fingers that granny's dinner service didn't arrive in a thousand fragments. Not so for people with multi-million-pound artworks. When these were moved around the world, shippers arrived with custom-made crates and packed pieces with the utmost care, so that when they reached their destination they were completely undamaged by the trip.

These works were so valuable and so cosseted that every mile they travelled was tracked by GPS. Plus, there were various customs checks and so on that required the production of a million and one bits of documentation. Consequently, shipping companies knew exactly what pieces they'd moved and, crucially, they knew the tiniest details of the journeys those artworks made. And they also had all the gossip about which works were being traded on the quiet.

The details they found for me about the Rothko's travels were illuminating. It turned out that Harrisons had indeed shipped the painting from the States to Sokolov's Chelsea mansion. But that was only one leg of its globe-trotting.

By the end of the day, I'd worked it all out. Or thought I had. My friendly art shippers, New York's finest at the

NYPD, Marcella, Clyde, and John Dixon all came up trumps and I could now explain the history of the Rothko, from the artist's studio to its theft from Sokolov's house. I knew who'd taken it, and why.

In some ways, this exercise had been for my own satisfaction. But if I wanted to have the leverage to keep Sokolov at bay, then I needed to understand how he thought and the way he'd reacted to the painting's exposure as a fake. How he'd insisted that he'd been ripped off and then demanded that I find the original, was key to that.

I would need to play on his weaknesses because despite what Becky had found, I knew that Yuri Sokolov wouldn't be stopped by the police. He was too slippery, his lawyers were too slick, and his influence was too far-reaching.

A bullet would probably stop him in a Russian back alley one day, when he'd finally run out of friends and crossed someone more ruthless than he was.

26

Eventually, I had everything I needed. I understood how the Rothko scam had worked and thanks to Becky, I had enough information to bring Yuri Sokolov to heel. He'd tried to control me via fear but soon he would realise that I had weapons of my own. I hoped that knowledge would outweigh his desire to torment me.

I called Joe.

"How's it going? Any more sightings of Sokolov's heavies?"

"Possibly. Although at more of a distance since Sam's arrival. Talking of which, now that I'm getting home late and he's moved in, I reckon some of our neighbours think that Ellie's kicked me out and got a new bloke. A younger, better-looking one at that." I could hear him smiling, less tense than he had been. "What can I do for you?"

"I need you to call a meeting at your office tomorrow afternoon. Get as many of your team along as possible and I'll make sure that Olga and Lucien are there."

"What are you planning?"

"I'll tell you how the theft worked, and why the painting

was taken. And I'll explain what we're going to do about Sokolov."

"You think we can do something?"

"I know we can. Trust me."

"I always do, Kate."

"And I've never let you down yet."

Next on my list of calls was Lucien. I would keep calling until he answered and I hoped he realised that. Then again, I could see why he might be hesitant, given what he'd dragged me into.

"What do you want?" Not the friendliest of greetings.

"How are you?" I thought I'd start off by being nice even though my patience was already spread thinly.

"Not great." He sounded wired on nerves and caffeine. "I haven't seen anyone, but I think I'm being followed." There was every chance he could be. Or maybe it was just paranoia.

"I wouldn't be surprised." I didn't mean to be unsympathetic but I hadn't called him so I could listen to his fears. I had enough of my own. "But I need you to do something. Can you and Olga meet me at Cathcart and Co in the morning?"

"I don't know her."

"Oh, come on," I snapped. "Don't mess with me. She came to the hospital when you were attacked. When I saw you by the river, you told me your alibi for the theft was that you were with a married woman. That was Olga, wasn't it?"

"Yes," he said quietly. "But I've known her a long time. And they're not married. It isn't what you think."

"You don't know what I think." He really didn't. Lucien assumed I'd twigged to their affair, but he had no idea of the other information I'd gathered. "I need you to come to the office and I need you to bring Olga."

"I can't do that. I'm in Amsterdam." He sounded panicky. "And he'll be keeping a close eye on Olga."

"Possibly. But it's important. This is almost over. And trust me, you'd rather be there than for me to send the Dutch police to pick you up. You have passports in other names?"

"Of course."

"Then use one of those. If someone is following you I'm sure you know how to lose them. But be there. I want to help you and Olga. Help all of us, for that matter."

By the end of the afternoon my head was swimming with details and weary from my niggling injuries, the slow task of cleaning my bedroom up and replacing my belongings, and from trying to keep the fear and the memories of the dead woman's face from my mind. I stretched and rolled my stiff shoulders. Flora was cooking dinner and I planned on taking a bath at her place and soaking away the lingering soreness in my muscles first.

The last email I saw was from Jim in Joe's office. He'd called in a favour from one of his former colleagues at the Metropolitan Police and got hold of the pathologist's report on the dead woman. I knew some of it from Spencer and Crieff's visit, but Jim warned me that it wasn't comforting reading. In fact, he suggested that I didn't look at it.

The document was at the bottom of the message and I thought about opening it, knowing that I needed to read it. But with a sigh, I decided it could wait. I had enough nightmares chasing me when I managed to sleep, without adding to them.

"Hello?" I answered the phone, lacking enthusiasm.

"Hi Kate, it's Becky. How's it going?"

"Okay. On the whole. Bit bruised still, a bit scared of being in my flat alone, but I'll be fine."

"Pete said he'd tried to send someone up to look after you. Maybe you should think about it?"

"No. In some ways it would be reassuring but all it would do is put off the moment when I have to tough it out on my own."

"I know what you mean." She paused. "I'm emailing over more information I've found. It's what you thought—drugs, people trafficking, illegal arms deals. He's got a finger in every corrupt pie going. And the witnesses who made complaints are hard to find. Most of them have disappeared although whether that's for their own safety or they've been disappeared I couldn't say. No convictions, obviously. His staff—probably the minders you had your run-in with—have criminal records too, and some of them look to be travelling on false papers, presumably because they wouldn't get into the country otherwise. It's horrible stuff, Kate."

"I thought it would be."

"And because you dented his ego he had someone beat you up? He's a psychopath."

"Probably. Nothing good at any rate." I sipped from the glass of water on my desk. "But it wasn't just the beating, Becky. Every time I think he's made his point, he comes after me again. He gets a kick out of knowing that people are scared and off-balance. I don't know what will be next."

"So what will you do with all this information?"

"What's the saying? 'Speak softly and carry a big stick'? Well, knowledge is power, and this is my stick. I'll find a way to use it to keep him at a distance."

"I hope it works." Becky didn't sound convinced.

"So do I, because I haven't got any other ideas."

After I'd hung up, I looked at the information Becky had sent over. It was exactly as she described, a catalogue of violence and crime. But it was the missing women in the forgotten police reports, some just teenagers, whose faces, sad and beaten, that would haunt my sleep that night.

Closing the files, I rested my head in my hands. Working out the story of the stolen Rothko forgery was one thing—it satisfied my curiosity, told me who was behind the theft and why, and how they'd worked the scam. And the more I read, the more I could understand the fear they'd felt. Justified fear, because Sokolov was no imagined monster. He was all too real.

"Have you solved the mystery of the dodgy painting?" Flora placed a plate of lasagne in front of me and I helped myself to salad. My new mattress was due to be delivered soon and I'd be able to move back to my flat. Remembering the way my pillows had been stabbed, feathers everywhere, I wasn't completely sure I'd sleep easily in my bedroom, but at least the broken glass had been swept away and the smell of bleach no longer clung to everything.

"I have. And now I know how to ensure that Sokolov watches his step in the future."

"Go on then. How did the scam work?" Flora poured me a glass of Shiraz and looked expectant.

"Ok, I'll try to keep it short." I took a mouthful of wine and began. "The stolen painting had perfectly good provenance on the face of it. Along with two others, it was bought directly from the artist in the 1950s by the Bernstein family." I explained about the house fire and how the paintings were thought lost. "When the Bernsteins died, they donated some of their art to MoMa in New York. The three Rothko paintings were ghosts—people knew of them but there were no records, they'd never been exhibited or catalogued and only one seems to have been photographed, but even then it's in the background and not particularly clear."

"Maybe they never existed at all? Or just that one in the photo?"

"You're very suspicious for a music teacher, Flora." I ate a forkful of lasagne. "I'm pretty certain that they did exist. Back then, at any rate. But a few years ago, the three paintings were 'found'," I said, using air-quotes for emphasis.

"How convenient."

"Quite. The story goes that after the fire they'd been put into storage because of their impractical size and were there for decades until finally someone opened the crates and realised what they were. This was the first part of the con. No-one really knows any details because it was claimed that the owner wanted to remain anonymous. That's not unheard of. All that's public knowledge is that they were a member of the Bernstein family. Anyway, all three were bought by the gallery Olga worked for. After a lot of restoration for the supposed smoke damage and the like, the gallery sold two and kept one back."

"The one Sokolov bought?"

"Exactly. Olga knew he wanted to buy a Rothko. It was a couple of years after the other two had been sold, but she knew there was still one in storage and so she brokered the deal."

"Knowing it was a fake?"

"I think so."

"What about the other two? Were they fakes?"

"No. I think there were three paintings and one was lost

in the fire, and when the surviving two were found, the third was faked. I mean, it was worth a lot of money and people are greedy. The person who inherited them might have been happy to go along with the story if it was worth their while. Maybe they didn't even know that the gallery had faked that third painting?"

"And the gallery in New York?"

"Closed when it was found they'd sold some other fakes. Some bore the fingerprints of a person who the NYPD were unable to identify. I've seen those prints and I've seen Olga's and I'm no expert, but they look a good match to me."

"So she was involved?"

"Yes. Maybe she sold other dodgy paintings to Sokolov? I don't know. Just like I don't know why she'd risk scamming him when she surely knew what he was like." I had a lot of the details but there was still much that was hazy.

"But you'll find out?"

"Possibly." I drank some more wine. "We're meeting at Joe's office tomorrow and I've told Lucien to make sure she's there. We can get at the truth and then decide a way forward."

"I don't know, Kate." Flora looked concerned. "It feels to me like all you'll do is provoke Sokolov. Surely it's best to just let it go and hope he forgets?"

"No." I spoke sharply. "He enjoys terrorising people and the only way to deal with him is to ensure that he's far more scared of me. Not physically, but I can promise to ruin him if he doesn't back off and I think that may be more effective."

Kolya rang me as I was getting ready for bed. I sent his Face Time call to voice only, not wanting to look him in the eye if I was economical with the truth. I still hadn't told him about the break-in or the dead woman, and I didn't plan to.

"Hello, my darling. How was your day?"

"Fine. Good to get back to work, you know?" My voice sounded unusually bright, even to myself.

"I saw my doctor today, he wants to move the surgery on my knee forward to next week. Will you come over to New York and play nurse? I'll get terribly bored stuck in my apartment while I recover."

"Next week? I'll have to check my diary."

"Okay. This sort of thing will be easier when we're living together." Kolya spoke as though this was a decision we'd already made. "We'll be able to have more time for each other. Even if I don't take the job in London, we don't have to always be in New York. We can look for a vacation house, perhaps? Pick an island somewhere warm."

"Maybe."

I realised then, with a wave of sadness, that this was not going to become the relationship that Kolya wanted. Although he'd been offered that amazing opportunity in London, what he would prefer was for us to settle down, for me to potter with my consultancy clients, give up my investigative work, and for him to start cutting back on his professional commitments. But now was not the time to tell him that I didn't want to spend my life wafting around as a semi-retired kept woman.

This was what the age gap between us really meant, I realised. He was looking forward to taking things easier while I felt I was just hitting my stride, at a point in my life, and my career, where I didn't want to be reducing anything. I wanted to keep working, keep travelling, keep chasing lost artworks, and keep enjoying that adrenaline.

27

At five am, I abandoned attempts at sleep and went running in a bid to work off some of my nervous energy. It was dark and the roads were quiet, save for a few other runners and early morning dog walkers. Mindful of the beating I'd taken last time I took a shortcut, I stuck to the main roads, avoiding the parks and back lanes.

Before I left for my flight to London and Joe's office, I skimmed through all the paperwork I had with me and read an email with more depressingly familiar information from Becky. Then I was ready to get going and get this over with. I had no idea where my day would take me so I was wearing jeans and boots I could run in, with a leather biker jacket that had avoided the ransacking of my wardrobe by virtue of hanging in the hall cupboard.

My phone rang once to announce the arrival of my cab. I picked up my overnight bag and looked at myself in the mirror, feeling more scared than superhero.

"Come on, Kate," I said to myself. "Time to go."

. . .

"Good to see you." Joe gave me a quick hug as I arrived at his office. "I think most of my colleagues are here. This Rothko might be a fake, but we all want to know what happened so it doesn't come back to bite us on the arse." Joe squinted at my face as he led me through to the conference room. "You're looking better."

"The bruising's still there. I've got a lot of makeup on today." I didn't want to talk about it. Now that the pain of my injuries had eased I'd almost forgotten them but my reflection still brought me up short sometimes. And when I looked at the bruises, the fear threatened to creep in and I had to push even harder to put it back into its box.

Other people started to arrive. Claire, Joe's PA, Jim, one of his investigators looking exactly like the cop he used to be, and Joe's business partners. Helen Wightman arrived from her gallery with some information she'd tracked down on Sokolov's recent purchases. She greeted me warmly and fussed about my bruises which seemingly weren't as well hidden as I'd hoped. I took my place at the head of the table, placing a bottle of water next to the neat stack of paper that constituted the grenade I was going to threaten to hurl into Sokolov's life.

Last to arrive, just as I'd given up on him, was Lucien de Bruin. He looked exhausted, and I felt a wave of sympathy at how complicated his life had become since we'd first talked on the riverbank. But not that sympathetic—somehow Sokolov knew we'd met and that had turned his fury in my direction. He was alone.

"Where's Olga?"

"She didn't turn up to meet me." He shrugged. "I hope she'll come straight here. I left a message on the phone she uses to contact me." He poured a cup of coffee and sat down, biting a fingernail.

"Go on then, Kate. You've got the answers. The floor's all yours." Joe smiled and leaned back in his chair, a smile which belied the worry in his eyes. But no matter what happened today, Sam would keep Ellie and their girls safe. I took a mouthful of water and began.

"As we all know, some more personally than others, Yuri Sokolov is a deeply unpleasant character. My job was over when his stolen painting proved to be a fake and I would have preferred to walk away then. But he's not a man who knows when to back off."

I paused, took a steadying breath, then outlined the attack on me, the break-in at my flat, and the dead woman at Leith docks. Itemised like that, it was chilling. Only Joe knew all of it and I saw the rest of my audience sit up straight and concentrate more, a couple wincing in sympathy as they imagined the impact that must have had on me.

"I wanted to find a way to make him back off and to keep him away in future. Not just for my own sake, but because he's a threat to anyone he perceives to have slighted him or threatened his rather fragile ego. That includes Joe and maybe more of you. However, what I've found is that although Sokolov is immoral, violent, and cruel, he's not involved in art forgery as far as I can tell. Not in terms of this Rothko, at any rate."

Everyone looked rapt, a couple were taking notes and, odd as it felt, I was starting to enjoy myself.

"I'll explain how the Rothko scam worked and then tell you a little more about the darker side of Sokolov so I can outline my plan to stop him threatening any of us again. Because he will. He's a sadist who likes to hurt and scare people." Lucien and I exchanged a look, both of us bearing the injuries to prove that.

First, I explained the history of the three Bernstein Rothko paintings, their decades as ghosts after the fire, before their convenient discovery in a storage locker and subsequent sale to the Leeman Gallery. I outlined Olga's career from corps de ballet to an assistant in that same Manhattan gallery, how she'd become involved with Sokolov, and how the fairy-tale had been over early in their relationship.

I paused again and wondered where Olga was. I wanted her here for her own good and I was beginning to worry about her safety.

"So, Sokolov wants a Rothko and Olga knows that the gallery has one in storage. She brokers the deal and the painting was sold for ten million dollars. That was a few years ago and it was a smart buy. Cheap enough to tempt him, not so cheap as to be suspicious."

"I thought the painting was a fake?" One of Joe's partners was already confused.

"Keep listening, she'll get there." Joe was sharp. "Just listen to the story for now."

"I'm sorry, there's a lot of detail." I smiled, careful to hide my displeasure. I'd spent days pulling all this together, and I was going to enjoy my Hercule Poirot moment. "Remember, you pay me a hefty retainer to be thorough about these things." I took another sip of water. "The shipper who brought the painting to London was Harrisons. As we all know, they're as straight as a die."

"I've never had a problem with them." Helen nodded.

"Nor me. And usually, they're very discreet. But I'm a good customer and so they checked their records for me. They did indeed ship the Rothko to Sokolov's house, but there was a tiny GPS tracker still tucked away in a corner of the stretchers. And that related to a journey two years earlier when Harrisons moved that painting to New York from Hong Kong. Only it was described as a Rothko copy on the paperwork with a declared value of a few thousand dollars. Harrisons were dubious but with the best will in the world, it's not their problem. They ship what they're told and any issues in terms of customs and duty are down to the owner."

"The third Rothko was a copy?" Claire asked.

"Yes. It entered the Leeman Gallery as a copy and left as the real deal. The two other paintings, the ones sold earlier, were genuine, but some works traded via that gallery have since been found to be forgeries and there are ongoing court cases."

"Did Olga know it was a fake?" Jim looked up from his notepad.

"She did." I looked at Lucien, wondering if he would contradict me but he just shrugged. My concerns for Olga were growing by the minute and I hoped she arrived soon. "And she took a cut of the selling price. Couple of million wasn't it?"

"Three."

"So why would Olga want to scam her boyfriend? They've been together for a few years so their relationship must be okay. He's loaded. If she needed money, why not just ask him?" One of Joe's colleagues was sceptical.

"It's not a good relationship." Lucien spoke quietly, his eyes fixed on the table. "He's abusive and controlling. He threatened that if she ever left him, he'd have acid thrown in her face." Everyone looked shocked. Everyone but me. It didn't surprise me in the least that he would threaten that, or that he would do it.

"We know he's violent. A PI contact of mine in the States tracked down a couple of investigations in New York following complaints from women he'd been seeing. One of them disappeared. The others withdrew their statements. He has expensive lawyers and people who will do his dirty work for him." I waved a hand in the direction of my face.

"But back to Olga. She took her cut, hid it away in a bank account somewhere, and fobbed Sokolov off with this fake. He knows nothing about art. It's just a way for him to show off his money and to appear more cultured than he really is. He isn't hard to fool."

"It was a good copy. If he hadn't decided to sell it, then none of this would have happened." Lucien looked up at me and shook his head.

"Quite. When he did, Olga realised her game might be spotted. She thought that if it was stolen, the insurers would pay out and no-one would ever notice."

"She didn't realise that we check things out carefully before we write cheques of that size." Joe said, and I drank some more water, my throat getting dry.

"But stealing a painting that big is tricky. Fortunately, Olga knew that she could call on you, Lucien. The pair of you had an affair in New York before she met Sokolov, correct?" He nodded. "So she asked you to help and because you were still in love with her you agreed, right?"

"Yes." He didn't look up at me.

"The difficult part was getting away with the painting. You're injured and not up to your usual activities so presumably you were outside and Olga dropped in through the skylight. Did she bribe the housekeeper to leave the window open?"

"Something like that."

"Once she'd cut it from the stretchers and rolled it up as

best she could, she shoved it out onto the roof and pulled herself back up and out. It's quite high but she's light and strong from all those years as a dancer. Did you get away through the gardens?"

Everyone turned towards him and Lucien nodded.

"And when you found out who the insurer was, you knew Joe would call me and so you appealed to my softer side, hoping that I'd feel sorry for you and find someone else to pin it on?"

"I thought you believed me." Lucien seemed quite put out. "Olga set up an alibi that she was visiting a friend. After we got the painting, we went to a cottage I'd rented in the New Forest and burnt it."

"So, what are you planning now?" I asked. He looked wary. "It's okay, no-one's coming after either of you for the burglary. It was a fake, so no pay out. No harm done, as far Cathcart and Co are concerned, right Joe?"

"Right." Joe didn't look completely keen on me letting Lucien off the hook, but he wasn't going to argue.

"Olga wants to leave him. The money from the Rothko is in a Swiss bank account and I'm organising new papers for us both. Then we'll just disappear." Lucien sounded more confident than I would have in the same position.

"Does Sokolov know about the two of you? He thought you'd taken the painting at first and he had your number. Did he get that from Olga? And you said people were following you in Amsterdam."

"Perhaps he heard my name from the police." Lucien shrugged.

"Or he knows that you and Olga are seeing each other." A chill ran down my spine. "Do you know where she is now?"

"No. At home, I think. Maybe she couldn't come up

with an excuse to go out. It's not always easy. He watches her." He looked scared, the same realisation dawning on him that I was feeling.

"Ring her."

He took out his phone and we all waited while he made the call. For all that he and Olga thought they'd been so clever, I suspected that Sokolov was a step ahead of them.

"Hello, Olga?" He sounded unsure. A voice spoke and then there was a click. He hung up and looked at us, white-faced. "I don't know who that was. A man with a Russian accent. He told me not to call again. And to forget about Olga."

28

The taxi was moving slowly, weaving from lane to lane without making any real progress, despite my pleas to find a faster route. With me were Lucien, ex-cop Jim, and Helen.

"Let us out here," I called to the driver as we stopped at yet another set of lights. I turned to Helen. "You stay in the cab. Wait outside with the others when you get to Sokolov's place."

"I'm coming too." Looking at Helen's stilettos and designer clothes I wasn't sure how much use she'd be.

"No. Just trust me and keep Joe and the others out of trouble." And with that, Jim, Lucien, and I set off on foot, dodging between people, cars and bikes, taking whatever shortcuts we found, running as fast as we could.

I had no plan for what we would do when we got to Sokolov's but I had a tight feeling in the pit of my stomach. Despite the fact that Olga was a scam-artist and a thief, and that her behaviour was the root of all that had happened to me, she was also a woman with an abusive partner and desperate for a way out. Sokolov was vindictive and I didn't think he'd think twice about carrying out his threats.

We hammered on Sokolov's gate and jabbed at the bell but no camera turned to look at us and no buzzer granted us admittance. Looking at Jim, Lucien nodded, the big man gave him a leg up and he was over the gate. Another few seconds and he'd opened it and the three of us sprinted down the path and up the steps to the front door. Jim was breathing hard, not as fit as he used to be, but he pounded on the door in his best police manner. No-one came, so he kicked it and the frame splintered.

In the hall, beige and tranquil, we looked around. Lucien went to shout out, presumably hoping Olga would hear him, but I laid a hand on his arm and shook my head. I wanted to get our bearings before we made any more of a commotion.

But no-one could have missed our arrival and one of Sokolov's tame thugs appeared from a room at the side, another from a door at the back of the hall. I recognised the second; I still had the bruises from his fists. Despite a wash of fear, I was pleased to see that the nose I'd broken at our last encounter wasn't healing neatly.

"Where's Olga?" My attacker glanced towards a door, the movement unconscious.

"I don't know anyone called Olga." It was the first time I'd heard him speak.

"The fuck you don't." I went for the handle and he grabbed my arm, yanking me backwards.

Jim planted a hand square in his face and booted the door open. I was beginning to realise what a useful man he was to have around. Lucien bolted for the doorway and Jim and I turned to face Sokolov's two henchmen.

. . .

The eyes of my attacker fixed on me, narrowing as though deciding that I wasn't going to get away from him again. Jim had his hands full with the other man who was swinging his fists and bellowing with rage. I turned towards my previous attacker, adrenaline fizzing within me.

I ducked his first blow, but he snatched at me, grabbed a fistful of my hair, and swung me round. Flailing, I managed to rake my nails down his face and he yelled and let go, sending me reeling. Regaining my balance, I grabbed at desperate split-seconds as I tried to look for a weapon. There wasn't much of use to hand and although I saw a sculpture on a side table, I didn't have time to grab it before he came at me again.

I ducked a couple of punches, his anger making him slower, but he caught my left arm, pulling me closer to him. Remembering what Pete had taught me in the boxing gym about self-defence and street-fighting, I stopped struggling. As he relaxed a little, my right fist snapped forward into his windpipe.

He let go of me, staggering backwards, gasping for air, and I followed up my advantage, left fist connecting with his jaw with a satisfying crunch and every scrap of strength I could muster. As his hand went to his face, and he was stopped in his tracks for a moment, I lashed out with my booted foot, immobilising him with a blow to the nuts that sent him crumpling to the ground.

Looking round at Jim, I saw him fell his opponent with a similar punch to the jaw. He didn't follow up with a kick to the genitals and the man didn't have deep scratches to his face. Obviously I fought dirtier than Jim.

Jim did, however, have the foresight to have cable ties in

his pocket and began lashing the two heavies to the banister with improvised handcuffs.

I paused for a moment, getting my breath back while I tried to get a feel for what was going on and wondering if there were more of Sokolov's minders lurking anywhere. I shivered in a chilly draught and smelling smoke, I followed my nose towards the rear of the house, down more taupe hallways into a drawing room that overlooked the manicured garden. I stepped through the open French windows onto a terrace and my jaw dropped.

In the middle of the lawn was a wide metal firebowl, perfect for sitting around on a cool summer evening, chatting with friends, drinking wine, and enjoying the crackle of logs.

At the moment, the fire was well ablaze and Yuri Sokolov was standing beside it, axe in hand. Next to him was a pile of paintings and he was chopping them into pieces and hurling them onto the fire. Sticking out, flames licking across the surface, was what appeared to be a Pissarro. Watching the canvas char and curl in the flames was like a punch in the gut, and I remembered how that felt.

"Stop! What are you doing?" I screamed, every instinct urging me to snatch the artworks from him while every bit of my sanity told me to keep as far away as possible from the psychopath with the axe.

"I'm burning these. All fakes. All the money I paid for these, that bitch stole from me." Sokolov punctuated his sentence by throwing an exquisite Degas sketch into the flames.

"Are you sure they're fakes?" It seemed quite a gamble to me. I glanced around, wondering where Olga was, and saw her peering out from the French windows, Lucien next to her with an arm round her shoulders.

"They must be. They're paintings she chose. What else would they be but forgeries?" He looked up, eyes icy, reaching for the next priceless artwork.

I didn't have an answer for him and I wasn't capable of reasoning with him, too shocked by what I was watching. Jim was beside me, a bruise already beginning to bloom on his temple.

Joe and Helen appeared too, their eyes wide as they registered the scene before them. Olga and Lucien stepped out onto the terrace, and the six of us stood there, unable to look away, as Sokolov, furious beyond all reason, hurled paintings onto the bonfire.

Knowing that this would be useful but not sure how at that moment, I took my phone out and fired off some photos and a video of the ranting Sokolov and his bonfire. Just in case. And it was a distraction from the horror of what he was doing. I wanted to stop him but couldn't see how, without putting myself in danger. He was a man possessed by his fury.

"Are they fakes?" I asked Olga quietly. She stood beside me, white-faced, bruised and shocked. She shook her head.

"No. The Rothko was. And a Miro. And a couple of Picassos at the house in the country. Those are all genuine."

Unable to watch the destruction of this inferno, works of genius going up in smoke, I stepped forward, ten feet or so from the fire. Sokolov glared at me from across the flames, axe in hand.

"Stop. Please don't do this. What if they're real?" I wasn't about to tell him categorically that they were. I didn't like to think about what levels of rage and violence that might provoke. I just wanted him to pause and calm down. “We can get them checked by experts. Don’t be hasty.”

“You bitch. This is all down to you. If I want to burn my paintings, I will.” He swung the axe in my direction.

I couldn’t fault his logic and stepped back. It was a tragedy from an artistic point of view but not worth getting hurt for. Not again, anyway.

I was holding my left wrist, the last punch I’d landed seemed to have jarred something. Punching that hard had probably been a bit rash given that I was already carrying an injury to that hand after my previous run-in with the same man. Still, better a sore wrist than the damage he’d have inflicted given the chance.

Sirens grew closer, screaming through Chelsea towards us. Lots of sirens. I looked at Joe and he shrugged.

“I told them to send everyone. I think we need everyone.”

He was probably right. The police, certainly, and the fire brigade would be useful. Olga could definitely do with an ambulance and the men cuffed to the banister might need more than a sticking plaster.

Me too, for that matter. I looked down at the wrist I was cradling and when I looked down I saw how fast it was swelling. The pain finally fought its way past the adrenaline that had been keeping it at bay and I started to shiver, queasy and cold.

“Are you okay?” Helen put an arm around my shoulders. I heard loud, authoritative voices, and police and paramedics appeared from the drawing room French windows.

“Yes. Yes, I think so. Apart from my wrist. I think I might have broken that.” And that was when I fainted.

. . .

When we arrived at the hospital, a motley collection of casualties with a lot of explaining to do, Jim began to fill in the police officers on what had gone down at Sokolov's, I curled up on a plastic chair in a corner. Helen sat beside me, patting my shoulder and muttering comforting words. Sokolov's heavies were being guarded by the burliest of the policemen and handcuffed to trolleys for good measure.

In between bringing me endless cups of disgusting sweet tea from a machine and shaking his head at the chaos his weekend had become, Joe paced up and down making calls to his business partners and to Ellie, warning her not to expect him home any time soon.

As I drank my third tea, resigned to waiting for hours until someone could do more than prod my wrist in an exploratory manner, Jim appeared, smiling, and handed me his phone.

"Call for you." He didn't say who it was and I pulled a face, not feeling up to conversation.

"Hello, this is Kate Carpenter."

"Shouldn't I be calling you Cassius? Jim tells me that the straight left that bust your wrist was worthy of any world champion."

"Hi, Pete." I sighed. "Please don't tell me that if I'd listened to you and had one of your guys with me then this wouldn't have happened. I know that but I'm not in the mood to hear it." I felt weary at the thought of a lecture, however well-meant it was.

"Okay, but I'm pleased those sessions in the gym meant you could deal with him yourself." Even though the phone line was patchy I could tell he was smiling, and I relaxed.

"Although maybe a bit more practice would have avoided the fracture."

"Possibly. The boot to the balls probably did more to stop him. But you didn't teach me that, it was all my own work."

"That's my girl. Look this is a crap line. Call me later. And take care."

And he was gone, leaving me smiling. Helen looked up from her phone and raised an eyebrow.

"Kolya?"

"No. Pete. Just wanting to see if I'm okay." I could see she was curious, fifteen years of friendship entitling her to be nosy, but all I knew was that the answers to any questions she had about my love life were more complicated than I could face at that moment. I leant my head against the wall and closed my eyes.

Once my wrist was examined and x-rayed and I'd been given a hefty shot of morphine to take the edge off the pain, I left Helen and went in search of Olga and Lucien. I found them a couple of cubicles down, huddled together. Olga's bruises were livid and she was twitching with shock.

"Hi." They both looked up as I spoke, Olga starting, her instincts on high-alert.

"Lucien tells me you saved my life," Olga began. I shook my head.

"I didn't do much. Just joined up a few dots."

"I wanted to leave him. I thought with enough money I could hide more easily, start a new life, and he wouldn't find me. And I wanted to help my family." She shivered and Lucien hugged her closer.

"He'd always have found you. Probably through your family. It's hard, nearly impossible, to completely start afresh. You would have to give up so much."

"You don't think I'm free now?"

"Maybe. You might be able to make him back off. He knows about the millions you conned him out of, but you know all sorts of shady information about him and that levels things up a bit. And his ego is out of control which gives us a lever. We'll talk about it later and make a plan. But I'm pretty sure we can keep him away from you."

"Thank you."

"Don't thank me yet." I swayed a little. "I'm going to go and sit down again but I need both of you to come to my hotel tomorrow. I'm booked in at the Chippenham. We'll put a few things in writing to keep you safe and then you can ride off into the sunset. Okay?"

They nodded and I went back to my chair and the latest cup of tea. The x-ray had confirmed the fracture I'd suspected. Apparently, it was complicated by the hairline crack I'd sustained after my last run-in with Sokolov's minder. This time I would be in plaster and needed to rest. The doctor looked at my notes when he said it and pointed out that his colleague had told me the same thing a week or so earlier. The pain of the injury diminished a little when Jim appeared, grinning, and told me I'd broken my opponent's jaw. That evened things up a bit, I thought.

29

Two weeks later

As I fidgeted with the thick folder of papers I held awkwardly in my right hand, Pete, newly arrived from the Middle East, went to take it from me but I shook my head. Helen twitched at the Hermes scarf she'd insisted should replace the NHS-issue sling to support my broken wrist and laid a hand on my good arm.

"Are you sure about this?" She glanced at the office door that led into the gallery I'd borrowed as the setting for this final act.

"Yes." I forced a smile. "I'll be fine. Nothing's going to happen to me, these guys will make sure of that." I nodded in the direction of Sam, who was no longer needed to guard the Cathcart family, and Pete. "All I need to do is ensure that he understands exactly how much power I have over his life. And he will." I tried to sound confident, hoping that I'd judged this correctly.

"All set?" Pete had a hand on the door handle, looking back at me.

"Absolutely. Let's do it."

A painting, Green Over Blue by Mark Rothko, hung at the far end of the long gallery. The rest of the walls were bare. The huge canvas, some seven feet tall, was the sole focus, lit by spotlights that only enhanced its drama and intensity. Having just negotiated the purchase of the painting on Jason's behalf, I'd rather relished the cruelty of setting up our meeting here.

In front of the Rothko was a padded bench where one might sit and lose oneself in its emotion and power. Sitting on that bench in an ill-fitting, too-shiny suit, his shoulders rigid with tension, was a man.

Waiting.

At the sound of my stilettos on the wooden floor, I saw him sit up a little straighter but he didn't look round as I walked the sixty feet or so towards him, flanked by Pete and Sam. About twenty feet from the bench, the two men halted, leaving me to cover the last few yards alone. I took my seat at the other end of the bench, crossing my legs and placing the leather folder next to me. I didn't hurry. Everything was exactly as I had planned and I was going to savour my victory.

"Mr Sokolov." I angled my body towards him a little, polite but unsmiling. He turned to look at me and nodded very slightly as he looked me over, all in black save for the bright scarf supporting my still-healing wrist. I saw his eyes narrow as though trying to spot the remnants of the bruises on my face.

"Miss Carpenter." Glancing over his shoulders, he took

in Pete and Sam who stood at ease, watching and waiting. "You told me to come alone."

"I did, didn't I? But as I don't trust you and I remember all too clearly the injuries your thug inflicted, I brought friends with me. They're not as obvious as your heavies but don't underestimate them, especially as they were both very angry when I was attacked. I wouldn't make any sudden movements if I were you." I smiled, polite yet cold.

"So, what do you want? Money? An apology?" He shrugged and I could see the anger simmering inside him.

"Not at all. You read the email I sent you carefully, as I suggested?"

He nodded and I imagined the look that must have crossed his face as he read it and realised just how much devastation I could wreak should I choose to.

I knew that Sokolov's business, his wealth, even his liberty, could be threatened and he might not care, but he was a narcissist and his ego was fragile. The photographs I had of him ranting like a madman and burning tens of millions of pounds' worth of art would open him to ridicule.

Olga told me his acceptance into the art world meant a lot to him because he felt it cancelled out his humble origins, the grubby way he'd made his money, and the seedier aspects of his life. People would laugh if they saw the photos of his bonfire. And then they would weep when they realised it was a genuine Matisse going up in flames.

If Sokolov wanted to maintain his position in that world, rather than become a laughing stock, then he really didn't want those images getting out to the wider world.

But I wasn't willing to risk people's lives based solely on my amateur assessment of someone's possible personality disorder and so I'd compiled a dossier comprising information from Olga and the documents that Becky had dug up.

By the time I'd finished putting all that together, I'd wanted to take a long, hot shower and scrub myself clean.

It wasn't just the polluted drinking water that killed two children at one of his housing developments in Siberia, or the drug cartels, or the hitmen, or the trades unionists who'd "disappeared". Nor was it the incriminating bank statements, emails and letters that Olga had photographed and sent to Lucien in a bid to provide herself with some insurance. It wasn't even the description of the injuries he'd inflicted on Olga; the broken ribs, the cigarette burns, the bruises where no-one would see them.

Individually, I could push all those horrors away, at least a little, but putting it all together, realising what utter scum he was, made me feel sick. As I filed all those documents into one place, I wept for his victims.

I'd checked with a senior police officer who'd worked with Jim, but he told me that, as I'd thought, this information couldn't be used due to statutes of limitations, jurisdictions and the like.

And so I'd sent an email, telling Sokolov a little of what I knew, attaching one of the more dramatic images from his bonfire and the statement of a brutalised teenage sex worker who'd disappeared after making a complaint to the police about him.

"Okay, you have all this so-called evidence about me. Or so you say. What now? The police won't be interested." He waved a dismissive hand and Pete cleared his throat. Sokolov's hand stilled.

"I have the information I showed to you and far, far more." I picked up the document folder and flicked through the papers inside. "Shall we run through a little more of it? The terrorists you're on such friendly terms with? The women you abused?"

"No. There's no need." He shook his head, starting to look just a little accepting of his defeat. "So what's your plan?" Nail-bitten fingers tapped on his thigh. I noticed a cluster of blisters on the back of his hand, small burns from his bonfire perhaps.

"I've got this information, and I still have people digging into your life so they will undoubtedly find more. Other people also have copies and because I'm a cautious person, for my own safety I don't even know who some of them are." Sokolov looked down, shoulders sagging just a little. "If anything happens to me, or anyone else involved in the business of your dodgy Rothko, the others will release this dossier to the press and the whole world will know about you. The tabloids would have a field day, don't you think? The photos of the burning paintings, the details of your seedy sex life, the images of your abused partner. The broadsheets would love the financial and political aspects, and those might go on to cause difficulties with your visa."

"This is blackmail," he hissed.

"Quite possibly." I shrugged. "I prefer to call it protection. If you come after any of us, I'll blow your life sky-high."

"And if I don't believe you?"

"Then you'd be a fool," I said sharply. "You might think I'm bluffing, that my hand's not as strong as I say, but it's mutually assured destruction, isn't it? All down to who blinks first. And I think you realise by now that I never blink first." Picking up the folder of papers he hadn't wanted or needed to see, I got to my feet. "And don't go looking for Olga. I don't think you'll be able to find her, but it would be a very unwise move to even try. I'll know if you do and I'll come for you."

And I turned on my heel and walked away, Sam and Pete falling in beside me. As Pete opened the door for me, I paused and looked back. Yuri Sokolov was sitting in front of the huge painting, head bowed, aware that the life he'd thought impregnable was in my hands, and that I had the power to make him pay for his actions, over and over again if I chose to.

EPILOGUE

The cafe near the Louvre was bustling. The vanilla-scented air was sent swirling by icy draughts every time someone came in from the wintry Parisian street. The two men at the table opposite me talked in low voices, the younger one looking a little furtive, the older more relaxed. The latter's eyes flickered in my direction and I returned my attention to the copy of Le Monde on the table in front of me, slowly reading a review of a new exhibition in my less than fluent French.

My phone buzzed and I glanced at it—a text from Joe confirming that he'd heard from Olga. I was relieved the plan I'd put in place was working. She and Lucien had disappeared with several million of Sokolov's dollars in a Swiss bank account, and the arrangement we'd made was that she would send a postcard to Joe's home address each month so that we knew she was safe.

This card was apparently from Crete, although we'd set up a network of people all over the world who could forward these on her behalf. The postcards had been distributed and on the appointed date, Olga would contact the next person on her list who would post it for her. No-one monitoring the Cathcart family's mail would know where she actually was. It wasn't the most sophisticated of systems, but it should work. If ever the card didn't turn up, I'd know to go looking for her.

Finding the family of the dead woman had been my next task after dealing with Sokolov. I'd hired a private investigator, unable to deal with the rawness of making those inquiries myself. It turned out that her name was Krystyna. She was from a small village near Krakow and had come to London to make a better life.

At first, she'd sent money home, telling her family about the circles she was moving in, the interesting people she'd met, but they'd heard nothing for a while and the arrival of my investigator on their doorstep with such bad news, albeit sparing them details, only confirmed their fears.

I'd paid for the repatriation of her body and her funeral, and forwarded some money that I pretended had been in her bank account here. I should have tried harder to help her when she was alive and I knew I'd always feel guilty, but doing the right thing too late, was better than not doing it at all.

It was a month since my meeting with Yuri Sokolov and I'd heard nothing from him. From what I gathered via art trade gossip, he was keeping a low profile and had been talking about spending more time in the country, stepping back a little from his hectic London life. I liked the sound of that. The thought of endlessly running into him at galleries and auctions made me wary, despite my brave words.

Now, it was November, my wrist was almost healed and I was back at work, in a cafe, eavesdropping on Julius Hoffman, a young South African man of German ancestry and distinctly Aryan appearance, who was trying to discreetly sell a Renoir painting that his grandfather had somehow acquired at the end of World War Two when he fled the victorious Allies.

The art dealer Hoffman was in conversation with had alerted me to the Renoir when it resurfaced. Both of us wanted to see it returned to its Jewish owners in the Netherlands. But Hoffman was already proving to be slippery and wasn't going to comply easily. He wanted to sell it and hoped that my dealer friend would be interested in buying it.

The older man glanced across at me again, and I nodded. He made his goodbyes and the two men left, separating at the door and heading away in opposite directions. Tapping a button on my phone, I switched off the recording app. From the fragments I'd overheard, I now knew a little more of the background to the painting and the young man's grandfather.

When the conversation was transcribed and signed off by my art dealer associate as a true record of their interaction, this would be another piece of the evidence I could leverage to persuade the young man that the most honourable way to deal with the Renoir was to return it to its rightful owners.

Gathering up my gloves and hat, I slipped the tiny electronic bug from beneath the two men's table and left the cafe. Looking down the street at the disappearing back of Julius Hoffman, I could already feel the anticipation rising as my plans started to fall into place. I texted Pete:

"I'm planning a pre-Christmas trip to South Africa after that looted Renoir I told you about. You up for it?"

A FREE KATE CARPENTER BOOK WHEN YOU JOIN MY READERS CLUB

One of the things I love about writing is my contact with readers. Join my Readers Club and I'll let you know about forthcoming books and other news. You can also download a free Kate Carpenter story—Vanishing Point—as a welcome gift from me. You'll find out more about Kate and how she first met Pete...

Just visit Vanishing Point novella

Reviews are hugely appreciated by authors and they help readers find books they might enjoy. If you have enjoyed Don't Blink and can spare a few minutes to leave a review, I'd be really grateful. Even a single sentence is helpful.

ACKNOWLEDGMENTS

Thanks to everyone who has advised, assessed and made suggestions for improving this manuscript. Special thanks must go to Karen Ball and Jane Badger for their editorial input, Barry Hutchison for his publishing advice, and a mass of people who've dispensed advice in books, blog posts and emails about the workings of the art trade.

In no particular order, a huge thank you to Sarah Painter, Martin Page, Caroline Copeland, Jane Anderson, Kelly Lacey, Helen Barrell, and Jacqueline Carrington Fallow. If I've missed you off the list, please don't be offended.

And of course, massive thanks to my husband, Malcolm, and son, Magnus, whose patience, wise counsel and plot ideas dreamt up over the dinner table are always appreciated.

ALSO BY VANESSA ROBERTSON

Trace Evidence

A missing woman

A life full of secrets

A friends in a desperate search

Art crime investigator Kate Carpenter is back in this fast-paced and twisty follow-up to Don't Blink, but this time it's an old schoolfriend she's searching for, not a priceless painting.

Although Kate and Beatrice were best friends, life has taken them in different directions. When Beatrice disappears without trace and her mother asks for help, Kate can't shrug off the pull of old loyalties and returns to her home town to track Beatrice down.

Finding her should be simple. Easier than finding lost paintings at any rate. And there are similarities — in both cases, Kate's just looking at the fragments left behind to see what they can tell her.

But Beatrice had a life full of secrets. Can Kate unravel the few clues she has and find Beatrice in time?

ALSO BY VANESSA ROBERTSON

Death Will Find Me

A former spy and her murdered husband.

Working in covert operations during World War One left Tessa with scars she still carries. Her hasty marriage is falling apart and after discovering her husband in a compromising position at a country house party, she tells him that she wants a divorce. But when James' body is found in a lonely stone bothy the next morning, Tessa is Inspector Hamish Rasmussen's only suspect.

Back in Edinburgh, links to another death force Rasmussen to enlist her help. Together they set off on a pursuit that once again brings Tessa face to face with the brutality of war and the desperate lengths that people will go to in order to protect those they love.

Will Tessa be able to prevent a final murder or will she become the killer's latest victim?

Published by Wild Justice Press

Printed in Great Britain
by Amazon

36744771R00138